A WAR OF MEMORIES

BUILTH WELLS
1939 - 1945

BUILTH WELLS & DISTRICT HERITAGE SOCIETY

First Published 2012
on behalf of
Builth Wells & District Heritage Society
by M.J. Morrison 6 Penybryn
Builth Wells, Powys. LD2 3LF

Co-authors:
Mal Morrison, Robert Warlow, Felicity Gill, David Bridgeman, Pat Power, Enid Jones, Dennis Jones & Jim Davies

Typeset in 9pt Verdana
Typesetting by Felicity Gill
Pagination by Mal Morrison
Printed in the UK

ISBN 13978-0-95151141-1

Gwen Davies 1928 - 2012

Gwen was the inspiration for this book. It was due entirely to her painstaking research and love of local history. We are eternally grateful to her for allowing us full access to her records, and we are truly sorry that her health failed before we could complete the compilation of this book.

It is fitting that it is dedicated to her memory.

Builth Wells & District Heritage Society, 2012

ACKNOWLEDGEMENT

We are deeply indebted to everyone who has supplied their memories for publication. Special thanks to Philip Jones, aviation historian, for information about plane crashes in the district, Brecon Library for access to their records, Michael Evans for his mother's autograph book and the wonderful sketches from Conti's Cafe, and so much more. And to Builth Wells Branch Royal British Legion for continual support and encouragement.

Book committee

Builth Wells & District Heritage Society

CONTENTS

FOREWORD

The inspiration for this book came from the late Mrs Gwen Davies (née Richards), who talked to the Builth Wells & District Heritage Society about her memories of the war years in Builth as a young girl. The talk was repeated several years later and a visitor asked if the talk was available as a pamphlet. This was the start and the book grew from there.

We are grateful to everyone who sent in their memories of these sad years and to those who sent in memories of other local people. These are personal memories and sometimes may differ slightly from the actual historical records.

We appreciate the photographs which people have allowed us to use.

Pat Power
Chair, Builth Wells & District Heritage Society

Autumn 2012

War Stories

Within the following pages are the stories of some of the servicemen and women from the district. We also have accounts from merchant seamen and residents of the town. The stories told here reflect indescribable suffering and heroism in some cases and the thoughts of the children of these grave times, who very probably had little understanding of the reasons for the shortages, the unexpected excitement of aircraft, both friendly and hostile, crashing in the district and the prisoners who were incarcerated in these parts (albeit perhaps in a very insecure manner) and spent much of their time toiling in the fields.

In the following pages we will read about the Land Girls, many of whom stayed here, the evacuees who maintain close links hereabouts, and so many stories from ordinary people who lived through these difficult years. Obviously many stories are missing. We could only print those we were privileged to receive following our appeal for war stories. They may not be factually accurate but they are people's memories and we offer them virtually unchanged apart from an occasional grammatical or spelling error. We sincerely hope we have done justice to these brave men and women.

Gwendda Home Guard (mounted section)

GWEN DAVIES

BUILTH WELLS DURING THE
WAR YEARS 1939 -1945

This is not intended to be an accurate, historical record of events but rather a personal recollection of Builth during the years 1939-45 as remembered by myself as a schoolgirl.

I think back to that long, hot summer of 1939 when a loaf of bread cost 4d and one could send a letter for 1d and it was delivered the next day; Builth streets were lit by gaslight and the milkman came to the door and poured the milk out of a tin can into your waiting jug; when there were 13 pubs, two policemen and a railway, and all the chapels were full with services morning and evening with Sunday school in the afternoon. Rev. Banner Mendus preached in Alpha, Rev. Caradoc Owen in Horeb, and Rev. William Griffiths in Memorial Baptist. Church Jones held sway in St. Mary's as Archdeacon. Llewelyn Morgan frightened the children as headmaster in the Council School and P.G. Davies in the County.

And the shops – at the end of the bridge, where 'Wyeside' is now, there were three shops, Charlie James with his watch repair shop, then Mr Howells had his boot shop smelling of real leather and dubbin, then came the 'Popular' sweet shop kept by Miss Madge Davies and her mother. 'Wyeside' was then a cinema known as the 'Kino' where we paid 3d to see such epics as 'Rin Tin Tin' and came home scratching from the Flea Pit. There were also two shops in Oaklands, one a grocer's shop kept by two sisters – the Miss Jones'. One was tall and thin with pince-nez and Miss Mollie was short and plump. Both always dressed completely in black. The other shop was in the front room of 28 Oaklands, kept by Mrs Percy Hughes, who sold aprons, lisle stockings, tablecloths and elastic.

This was a time when Builth had a railway and a goods yard, when Station Road was a hive of activity with a bus station, two coal merchants, a stone mason, butcher's shop, wool stores, timber yard, cycle shop and a café as well as the furniture and grocer's shops. Pendre and Western Grove were green fields and Frank Morris was chairman of the U.D.C. Many will have their own memories of our town in those far-off days, but think now of the boys and girls who were still in school in that September who five years later returned, prematurely aged, having seen the horrors of war and fought in places that they had hitherto only known as names on a map – 19 of those boys didn't return at all.

Sunday 3rd September 1939. These memories are my own personal ones, some of them checked by reference to others and some of them perhaps coloured by imagination.

It was a lovely sunny morning, I went to Chapel as usual, and came home to find my mother in tears, because Mr Chamberlain hadn't received a reply to a letter he had written to one Adolf Hitler, and we were "At war with Germany". The house was full of soldiers in khaki, there were only four, but it was a small house. They were my eldest brother Gwyn and three mates who were in the T.A. and had actually been called up days before war was declared. They now had to report for duty.

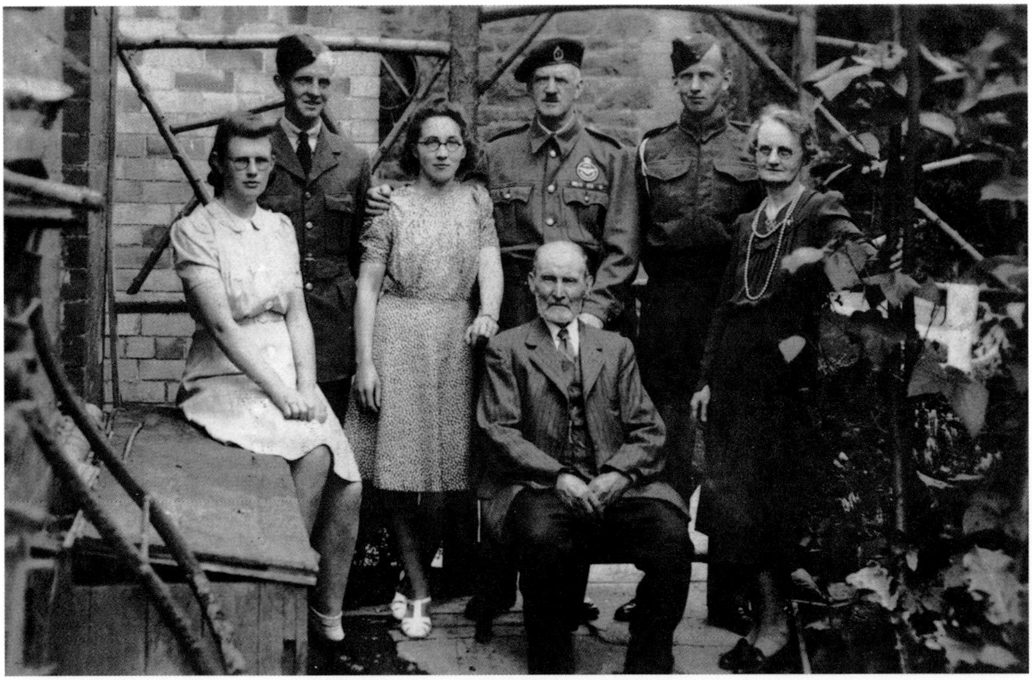

Gwen Davies (far left) and family

In Horeb Chapel that morning the minister, Rev. Caradoc Owen, said the following words: "Europe will become a continent of bloodshed on a far greater scale than that of the 1914-18 war. Nevertheless the gospel of love and peace will be preached, though the whole world will be filled with the sounds of war, enmity and hatred." Profound words. In Llanganten Church the congregation heard the voice of Mr Chamberlain broadcasting to the nation as the vicar had, with great foresight, taken his wireless set with him to church.

What followed next was known as the 'phoney war' as nothing seemed to happen. Everyone said "It will be all over by Christmas". Little did we know what we were all in for. Words like Blitzkrieg, Quisling, and Lord Haw-Haw were not yet in our vocabulary and fortunately we had not heard of Belsen, Dachau, Auschwitz and Hiroshima. We sang 'Run Rabbit Run', 'The White Cliffs of Dover' and 'We're going to hang out the washing on the Siegfried Line' along with Vera Lynn.

The face of Builth started to change slowly. Evacuees came. First we had mothers and children under five from Bootle – one of the not so salubrious areas of Liverpool. We had never seen women going into pubs on their own and they had never seen a town like Builth – it only had <u>one</u> chippy! To say we didn't get along was an understatement. They returned to Bootle after a few weeks saying that they would prefer to face the bombs and the wrath of Hitler rather than stay in Builth. The 'blackout' was enforced, with A.R.P. wardens armed with a tin helmet, armband and truncheon, shouting at every shaft of light "Put that light out".

Ration books and identity cards were issued. Everyone had to 'register' with a grocer and butcher, etc. to get foodstuffs. There were 'points' for tinned goods, dried fruit, jams, jellies, etc. But the weekly ration for essential foods per person was:-
2 oz. butter, 2 oz. lard, 2 oz. marg., 2 oz. cheese, 4 oz. sugar, 4 oz. bacon, 4d worth of corned beef and 8d worth of meat. Later the meat ration was increased to 1/- worth.

There was one way grocers could get dried fruit and that was by buying it in sacks from Southern Ireland, but it had to have sugar added first. To make a birthday cake one had to save up the fruit for many weeks. Furniture was sold on dockets, and the dockets were issued only to newly-weds, who had enough to furnish one room and 10 square yards of lino. Growing children were allowed to have a single bed when they grew out of a cot. Everything else had to be second-hand.

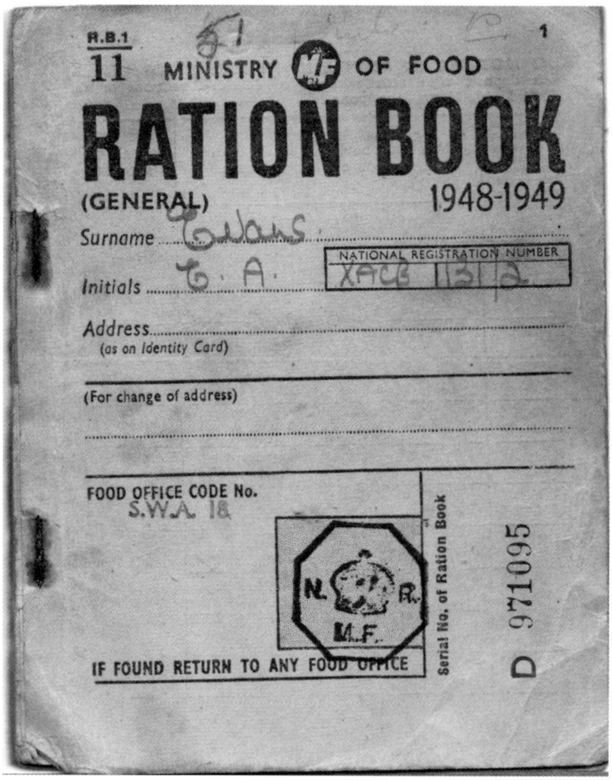

Rationing continued well after the end of the war

Clothing coupons were issued to obtain clothes. The slogan was 'Make Do and Mend'.

Gas masks were issued and had to be carried at all times. Before lessons started in school all children had to have a gas mask practice and sit for several minutes with the masks on.

All names of towns were removed. No signposts were to be seen. It was particularly difficult when travelling by train as one could not see which station one was at, and especially difficult at night when there were no lights anywhere and only a very small torch was allowed.

Church bells were to be rung only in time of an invasion.

Petrol was severely rationed, only farmers and business vehicles had petrol coupons.

Everything aluminium was handed in to make weapons. Women gave their saucepans to be turned into munitions, some gave jewellery, even their wedding rings, for the war effort. The railing disappeared from The Groe. Children couldn't play on the beaches around the coast as they were mostly mined and blocked off with rolls of barbed wire.

But this was nothing compared with the heartache caused by the call-up of the men for military service. They were called up in age groups, every man from the age of 18 was required unless medically unfit or in a 'reserved occupation'. In this area few men other than farmers were exempt. Women were left on their own to bring up the family. Later women as well were directed into the forces or munitions factories. In Builth premises were requisitioned. All halls and large premises were taken over by the army.

The Lion Hotel became an officers' mess. Ashfield House was an office and had an armed guard on the gate, day and night.

The 'Queens Vaults', later Harley's paper shop, and the Baptist school room were taken over by the Home Guard. The Church Hall was a sergeants' mess and Alpha school room was a canteen run by the Y.M.C.A. and W.V.S. Twelve acres of The Groe was taken by the army to park vehicles, for which they paid £40 per annum, and the bowls pavilion was rented for £26 per annum.

Builth Home Guard

Evacuees: Soon evacuees started to arrive. 150 unaccompanied children had to be housed. Mr Llew. Thomas (Monocle) was in charge of the operation with scouts and guides helping. They were fed on arrival at Morris' Café. One week later 10 had returned home. They were mostly from the London area and were very homesick. In 1941 the London County Council sent a cheque for £9 to give them a party.

H.T. Price's Garage (now Cee Gees) and Captain R.J. Owen's Garage were to be used as first aid posts. Lady Barstow, Chapel House, and Mrs Thomas, Pencerrig, offered their large upright cars as sitting ambulances. Miss Grace Phillips and Hon. Mrs Barnard, Caerberis, called a meeting in the Greyhound Hotel for women to form a group to make comforts for the troops. They knitted hundreds of balaclava helmets, mittens and socks.

Blackout: No lights were to be visible from the air so curtains had to be lined with blackout material, or blinds had to be fitted to windows. When an outer door was opened it had to be opened very little and shut immediately, otherwise an A.R.P. warden would be shouting. Car headlamps were fitted with shades so that the light was thrown only a short distance. Everyone carried a torch but with a very small light. Shops were to close early – 6 pm on Monday to Friday and 7 pm on Saturday – and shoppers were encouraged to shop in the daytime to avoid being out after dark. Kerbs were painted white and the gas and electricity boards were to be asked to paint the lamp standards white.

Item from the Brecon & Radnor – "Owing to the blackout restrictions no pleasure fairs were held on The Groe but it was reported that on Fair Days all the seats up The Groe were taken by 9 pm and the blackout was really appreciated".

Everyone had to 'Dig for Victory' and all flower beds gave way to vegetable patches. Mr Occy Samuel sent his tractor to the County School to dig up 1½ acres at the bottom of the playing fields and gave the seed potatoes to be planted there by the pupils in their free lesson time.

Air raid shelters sprang up all over town, fortunately they were never used. But a formidable air raid shelter was made in the cricket field by Mr Jack Lewis, Radnor House, with some help from local youths. But the B & R suggested that "more help should have been given from those in the vicinity who might be expected to use it". If an air raid had taken place shoppers in the main street would have taken refuge in the cellars at Hamer's Store, Vaughan Vaughan's and Weale's shop.

In July 1940 50 stirrup pumps were purchased by the Urban Council and distributed around the town. About 12 months later Mr Fred Turner wanted to know whose responsibility it was to keep the pumps in order as they were getting rusty.

Local land army girls

After an appeal by the town crier, Mr Joe Davis, volunteers filled 1000 sandbags with sand from the Aber Pool for use at the hospital.

A tremendous amount of money was collected in Builth for the war effort. One of the first schemes was the 'Penny-a-Week' Red Cross scheme. The town was divided into 12 areas and a collector appointed for each. Mr Glasscodine, stationmaster, organised our street. Later this was done by Mrs Joyce Waters. One shopkeeper wanted a receipt for his penny, each week! Then there were special weeks such as 'Spitfire Week', 'Comfort for the Troops', 'Aid to Russia' and 'Aid to Air Raid Victims in London, Cardiff and Swansea'. The 'War Weapons Week', which had a target of £20,000, reached a staggering £58,883/4s/3d from 31st March to 7th April 1941. This was from the Builth district alone.

BUILTH WARSHIP WEEK.

MARCH 23rd to 30th.

REMEMBER SINGAPORE!! REMEMBER JAVA!!

MEN We Cannot Replace.
SHIPS We CAN Help To Build.
The Navy Guards Our Food.

£40,000!

This Objective can only be achieved if everyone combines whole-heartedly.

LEND TO SAVE! HOARD, YOU'RE SUNK!

Come On, Builth!! Give Hitler a Knock-out with a Smashing Result.

This Space is donated by CHIPPENDALE HOUSE.

Every event held in the town was in aid of some fund to help the war effort. One of the most amusing was named 'Baccy for the Boys' and a weekly dance was held in order to send tobacco and cigarettes to the local boys in the forces. Admission was 6d rising to 9d later on in the war. There were weekly whist drives held in 'Jane's Parlour' on The Groe, these were in aid of the Red Cross. The Catholic school children, who were evacuated together with their teachers from Liverpool, organised dances in the scout hut, and the money from these dances was used to send parcels to local boys at Christmas time.

Possibly the most stupendous effort was made by the local ladies who collected War Savings every week. Each road had a collector and every house was called on once a week and the householder would buy savings stamps for the war effort. The main organisers were Mrs Charles Roberts, Miss Gwlithin Phillips and Mrs Mary Luther Davies. The last two went to Buckingham Palace after the war in recognition of their services. The organiser for the County School was Miss Hough who collected many thousands of pounds – each form competing with the others for collecting the most.

Home Guard: One area in which possibly the most people were involved was the Home Guard. This was first formed in 1939 and was then known as the L.D.V., which stood for Local Defence Volunteers or Look, Duck and Vanish. They really did do their first training with broom handles. Later they were issued with proper uniforms and rifles and got down to serious training with the army on the Epynt Range. They were first under the command of Mr Walter Weale, draper, with Lord Trevethin as Area Commander. Mr Weale was succeeded by Mr Charles Roberts, postman. The Builth area was divided into platoons with Major Russell in charge of Llanelwedd and Mr Rylands in charge of Builth Road. Later women were able to join and received instruction in Morse code and radio signals. Practise in the use of field wireless was held in the field where Western Grove is now, the instructor was Mr Colbren of the Electricity Board. The women did not have uniforms but wore huge Bakelite badges and received a certificate of thanks signed by Sir Grigg at the end of the war.

All the entrances to Builth were guarded by members of the Home Guard and today one can see the remains of gun emplacements which were situated at each entrance to the town. These were made by the Ministry of Defence. The man in charge of the workmen was a Mr Young, who came with his family to live in Builth, and was here right through the war years. The Young family came from Deal, Kent and both son and daughter married into local families. The M.o.D. office was at the entrance to the cricket field.

The dugouts were situated:- one on the right-hand side of the road opposite the entrance to Caerberis; one on Hospital Road; one at the top of Brecon Road; one on Llanelwedd rocks and one on Hay Road by the entrance to Woodlands. I asked Mr Charles Roberts why the bridge was not guarded and he said that it was mined and would have been blown up in the event of an invasion. The men in the Home Guard took their duties very seriously and would have played a major role in the defence of the country if called upon to do so. They trained hard and put in many hours, and sometimes weeks, of practice. They were mostly middle-aged men who were doing a full day's work as well.

Builth Wells Royal Observer Corps

Observer Corps: These were the men who manned the observation post at the top of Brecon Road. They plotted the flights of planes, both German and Allied, which flew over Builth, and the post was manned day and night, the men being on duty for 2, 4 or 8 hour shifts. Some of these would do an 8 hour night duty and then go straight to work without a rest. The hut was very small and was heated by a very smelly wood-burning stove. Mr Archie Vest, who kept the local fish and chip shop was an Observer and used to be very popular because he always brought with him a huge packet of fish and chips to consume during his stint. Sometimes the combination of the stove and the chips became somewhat overpowering.

A.R.P.: Then there were the men of the A.R.P. (Air Raid Precaution). They were the ones who wore tin helmets, A.R.P. armbands, carried torches and shouted "Put that light out" every time someone opened a door or put a light on before drawing the curtains. They rated in popularity somewhere about the same as traffic wardens do today. One little tale told at the time concerned Mr Wallace Jones. Wallace was a little man who had a photographer's shop opposite the Drovers, and he ended most sentences with "Mun". One dark night Wallace, who was an air raid warden, was approaching the Irfon Bridge, which was being guarded by one of the Home Guard. As Wallace got near the guard called out "Halt, who goes there?" "It's me, Mun", said Wallace. "Halt, who goes there?" said the guard again. "It's me, Mun", said Wallace. "Halt, who goes there?" said the guard for the third time. "Don't be silly, you know me, Mun", replied Wallace. Silence for a short while, then the Home Guard said "If you don't tell me who you are, Wallace, I'll bloody well shoot you".

Then there was another story about the time when a German plane crash-landed in the Hundred House area. The crew baled out, but unfortunately one was killed and was buried in Glascwm churchyard. After the war his family took him back to Germany for burial in his home town. However, one of the German air crew landed safely and was running up the main road when he was met by a Home Guard in uniform walking with his girlfriend. The German immediately put up his hands in surrender, shouting "Kamerade", at which point the brave Home Guard man took to his heels and ran off in the opposite direction, leaving the girlfriend with the German! What happened next is not recorded.

Women in War: While the men were in the forces the women too were doing their share for the war effort. I have already briefly mentioned the canteens that were run by the W.V.S. and the Y.W.C.A. The first to open was in Alpha Church school room and an evening was allocated to each of the churches and chapels to supply and serve tea and refreshments to the soldiers stationed in the town. As the food available was somewhat boring, consisting mainly of reconstituted dried egg, cheese and pickle sandwiches and jam tarts, the main attraction for the troops was a place that was warm, friendly and somewhere where they could read or write letters home. In fact a few of them had to get the women to write the letters for them as they were unable to write easily. Other women spent their spare time knitting socks, gloves and balaclava helmets, rolling bandages, etc. Then there were those who took evacuees into their homes, sometimes four or more, as brothers and sisters refused to be parted. One lady, a Mrs Gough of Brecon Road, had as many as 50-60 evacuees at various times throughout the war and was eventually awarded the B.E.M. Some of the children she took in remained in Builth and married here. After the bombing of London and Cardiff many wealthy Jewish families bought properties in Builth and evacuated their women, children and retired parents to the town. The children went to the local schools and proved to be very bright and, especially in mathematic subjects, far in advance of the locals. In fact some of them were in advance of the teachers! It would be interesting to know what mark they made in the world. Very few of them have returned to Builth since the war. It was quite a difficult time for women, most of them had previously relied on their menfolk to make all the decisions, very few had gone to

The Gough family and some of their evacuees

work after marriage, and now they were left to bring up children on their own. They had control of money for the first time and if single they were directed into the forces or factories. Mothers had to make nourishing meals out of meagre rations, using such things as dried egg and Spam, and although rationing was nowhere as severe as in cities there was still a shortage of sugar and tea, etc. It took a lot of juggling with the rations to feed a family, and every household tried to save something to make 'special' treats for when the men came home on leave.

Girls who perhaps had never travelled further than Llandrindod were sent miles away from home to strange places. It was, for some, the most adventurous time of their lives. Women's Lib. had set in and things were never the same again.

Women's Land Army: But if the local girls were in short supply, this was compensated for by the moving to Builth of the Women's Land Army. A hostel to house these girls, who were mainly from cities, had been built near White House Farm. The huts were later to house German and Italian prisoners-of-war, who were also to work on the farms in the area.

Land Army girls with Builth Wells railway station in the background

The Land Girls came from all walks of life – some of them thought that milk came out of a bottle. But they did a magnificent job and were a tremendous help to the farmers who had to plough up every available acre of land to supply food. The girls learnt to drive tractors, plough fields and milk cows, in short everything a man could do, and many of them settled down so well to country life that they never returned to the cities. Some married local men and even brought their parents to live here as well.

Sometimes on Sunday nights they used to organise beauty competitions in the cinema, then known at the 'Kino'. The Land Girls mostly came 1st, 2nd and 3rd!

An interesting piece of information was that Miss Hilda Vaughan, the author, better known as the wife of Charles Morgan, was one of the first organisers of the Land Army in the First World War. When the Second World War broke out she returned to Builth, which was her home town, and helped to organise the Land Army in Brecon and Radnor.

Soldiers stationed at Builth: Some of the first soldiers to be stationed in Builth were the Enniskillen Dragoon Guards who came direct from the beaches of Dunkirk in June 1940. Some of them were stationed in Ashfield House, Park Road and we had many of them in for hot meals and baths and we heard with fascination their many tales of escape and rescue by the 'little boats' from Dunkirk. One soldier told of his carrying of gold bars from a bombed bank some distance from the beaches. One by one the bars were thrown away as they got heavier and heavier. He hung on to one right to the end and as he tried to swim to a rescue boat the last one was thrown as it was too heavy to swim with and it was the gold bar or his life.

At this time Mr Bligh of Cilmery Park owned a small lock-up shop in the High Street, next to Chippendale House. It was empty in 1940 and Mr Bligh offered it, free of charge, to the W.V.S. to use as a headquarters. The soldiers had come from Dunkirk with their old uniforms in tatters; they had been issued with new uniforms but without their insignia and stripes, etc. It was in the little shop that the ladies of the W.V.S. used to sew these on for the soldiers. The shop was also used as a distributing and collecting point for all the garments which were made by the local women for the forces.

During 1942 the Builth Urban District Council as part of Warship Week adopted two naval vessels, H.M.M.L. 137 (seen here) and H.M.S. Cordela, a trawler armed with one 12 pounder A.A. Gun. A plaque on the outside wall of the Lion Hotel commemorates this.

A letter was received by the local council, from the Home Secretary, with a request that, as soldiers were stationed in the town, the cinema be opened on Sundays to prevent them being bored. Councillor Llew. Jones, a religious gentleman known locally as Hallelujah Jones, voiced strong objection to this, saying that it would desecrate the Lord's Day and lower the moral tone of the country! A letter from the council to this effect was sent to the Home Secretary. However, the cinema was opened on a Sunday, if not for film shows, certainly for concerts. It must be remembered that there were no halls available for entertainment as the Strand Hall was a factory and all Sunday school rooms had been requisitioned, although there were many 'Sacred Concerts' held in the chapels, mainly Alpha and Memorial Baptist.

Army Camps: The biggest impact on the town was when the army camp was built at Pendre. This meant that the population of the town was doubled and sometimes trebled overnight. The building of the camp took place in 1940-41. The site was cleared, drains and other facilities put in and the wooden huts erected and the Kent Yeomanry were installed in 1941.

The townspeople did a wonderful job of making these men feel welcome. They invited them into their homes, supplied hot meals, baths and evenings by a real fire. Many friendships were forged and several marriages took place between local girls and soldiers over the ensuing years. The Land Army girls were very popular too. It is quite common now to find an elderly man wandering about the Pendre housing estate trying to figure out where his wartime hut used to be.

The 'Kino' was packed every night, showing films like 'Dangerous Moonlight' and 'Mrs Miniver'. There were dances in the Drill Hall and even the Market Hall, which had a stone floor and was heated by a brazier in the centre of the room. The Drill Hall during the day was used for training by the Home Guard, so the floor was not exactly ideal for dancing. Entertainment was not given a high priority in Builth during the war!

Polish soldier

Apart from British forces we had Polish, Canadian and American troops stationed in Builth. They caused no trouble until at one time there were white American soldiers at the Pendre Camp and black American soldiers, under canvas, at Pencerrig Camp. There was so much animosity between the two that they had to be kept apart. The black soldiers were only allowed as far as Llanelwedd Hotel, not able to come into the town, and the white Americans not allowed over Builth Bridge – a guard being stationed at each end. When the white Yanks moved out the black soldiers were allowed into the town and caused no trouble at all.

I have already briefly mentioned that the Strand Hall was used as a factory during the war years. It was, in fact, taken over by Harrison, McGregor and Guest (Halls Telephone Accessories) and it was here that they made parts for the famous Bofors gun. It deserves a mention if only for the fact that it was the reason for our having Councillor Harry Fricker living in Builth. Mr Fricker came from London in 1943 as a designer/draftsman to work in the factory and he designed the part of the gun that was made in Builth. He married local girl Josephine Owen, daughter of Captain R.J. Owen, the town clerk, and settled in the town eventually becoming town mayor.

Many local people worked in the factory, mainly women, and it was so successful that a deputation of workers wrote to the Council and the Chamber of Trade asking for their support as they had decided to carry on with the factory when the war ended. They would have liked to make farm machinery. I believe that this idea did not materialise owing to the lack of parking space around the hall and some of the work force went to

Llandrindod to work in a factory which started up there making machinery, but it did not last long.

Mr Conti in his shop

There was one person living in Builth who was in a different category from most, and that was Mr Conti of Conti's Café. Mr Conti was Italian born and came to Britain in the 1930s. He was a naturalised Briton and had become a popular member of the Builth scene. His mother, who lived with him, spoke little English and had to report as an alien. She always dressed in black and the family had difficulty in preventing her cutting up the blackout curtains for skirts.

When Italy entered the war Mr Conti thought that there might have been some antagonism shown towards his children in the school. But apparently not one word or any hostility was shown to any member of the family throughout the war years.

Mr Conti was eternally grateful to the people of Builth for this and through the war he sent parcels, at his own expense, and unknown to most people, to all the local men serving in the forces. He was also concerned that his small café, which was always full of soldiers from the camp, would not have room for the local boys when they came on leave, so he opened up his own sitting room for them and kept special treats, like favourite brands of cigarettes and biscuits, for the local men. He was a fine man and greatly respected.

Builth Wells auxillary fire service

There were many other groups in Builth operating during those war years that have not been mentioned, such as the Air Training Corps, the Y.M.C.A. and the Fire Brigade - this was an especially dangerous job as the firemen, who were volunteers, were called on to fight fires after bombing raids in Bristol, Swansea and Cardiff.

Many women, with or without nursing experience, worked in the local hospitals, or in the Military Hospital at the Rock Park Hotel in Llandrindod, this hotel having been turned into a hospital at the outbreak of war.

When hostilities seemed to be coming to an end, the Italian and German prisoners of war who were held in the hostel previously used by the Land Girls were allowed out under guard to work on farms and gardens in the area and were also allowed out to church. It was an unforgettable moment to hear the German PoWs singing 'Silent Night' in German in a carol service held in the Baptist Chapel one Christmas Eve. Each man sang with tears streaming down his face, and so did all those who heard them.

German prisoner of war on a local farm

Bernard Allen

Evacuated to Builth Wells

It was summer 1939. I was eight years old and living in Birmingham - a large industrialised city. Everybody was talking about war (whatever that meant?). The way the adults talked, it certainly wasn't good; apparently, it was something to do with Germany. The only thing I knew about that place was that most toys were marked 'Made in Germany'.

Everybody was being issued with gas masks - horrible smelly things made of rubber, which you put over your head and which covered your face so that you could hardly breathe. In fact if you had your hand over the holes at the front you couldn't; one did this to test no air could get in through the sides! There were special 'Mickey Mouse' style masks for the very young children, and the big ones which you could put a baby completely inside. All these were in case the Germans dropped things full of gas on us from planes flying over.

All the young men were being called up to serve in the Army, Navy and the Royal Air Force. Sand bags were piled up around doorways of important buildings, such as council and government offices. People were given 'Identity Cards', with a number which showed where you came from, and how many were in the family.

Preparations were also under way for all children under a certain age, usually 14 years, to be evacuated from the big cities, which were most likely to be bombed, to the country and the outskirts of towns, which were comparatively safe. Whole schools were packing in preparation to leave. My name was down to leave also, with my school; something I didn't relish at all as I remember. Eventually, the schools started to move out. (I had got round my mother and persuaded her to let me stay). I, and one or two pals, who also were not going, went up to watch them leave, along with the teachers. The schools would be closed. All those children boarding the coaches had their little cases, or carrier bags, and a label with their name and the name of the school tied to their coats, and off they went to the railway station. With all the children leaving and the men going into the forces the town seemed very quiet and almost deserted. Very few people had cars in those days - even in the cities. Bread, milk and coal, etc., was delivered by horse and cart.

My new-found freedom was not to last for long. The lady who lived next door to us was Welsh and came from Builth Wells. Her family still lived there and quite often came to stay for a holiday - especially their elder daughter, who was the same age as my elder brother. They often played together when she was there. By chance she was there at the end of August 1939 and due to go back to Builth Wells very soon.

On the afternoon of September 1st I was playing in the street outside my aunt's when my brother came to fetch me. He said I was to go home to pack. My parents and the lady next door had decided I could go back to Builth Wells with her niece the following day. So on the morning of September 2nd 1939 Grace and I caught the bus from Birmingham to Llandrindod Wells, where we caught the local bus to Builth Wells.

For me as a child holidays had been a rare event. They consisted mostly of a day trip on a coach, or charabanc as we called them in those days. I woke up on that first morning to the sounds of the birds! On looking out of my bedroom window I could see nothing but hills all around, instead of roofs and back yards. One thing especially I could see was the site of Builth Wells castle, where I was to spend a lot of my time playing and exploring.

In spite of the inevitable homesickness I soon made friends of my own age, and before long I knew Builth Wells almost as well as any of them. We would cover many miles across fields and climb hills. There was less restraint in the country, so most of our forays around were without supervision, other than being told not to go by the river. Although there was a place up The Groe where, when the river was low, we could wade across to the other side.

Apart from the eldest daughter of the family who had brought me to Builth there was another daughter, who was three years older than me, and quite a tomboy! Her word was law and woe betide anyone who went against her. She was quite big, and always took the lead in whatever we did, nobody argued with her. On the other hand she was fiercely protective of anyone in her gang!

The lady of the house - 'Auntie Gladys' - was fairly strict and one did what one was told without question. But her husband - 'Uncle Mac' - always stood up for me saying "Leave the lad alone". One of my jobs was to take the little hand cart to the farm to fetch manure for his allotment where occasionally I was allowed to help out. Another of my jobs was to collect logs for the fire and I would travel quite a distance with my little hand cart to places where driftwood or broken trees provided the necessary wood.

We did not see much of the war in Builth Wells - only in the newspapers and the wireless. Whenever there was a mention of Birmingham and the air raids, it was an anxious time, until I heard from my parents to say they were safe. There were times when the air raid siren would sound in Builth Wells - but only for practice, and occasionally we would leave school, wearing our gas masks with orders to go straight home to see how long it took us!

Bernard (R) with Norcliffe Lloyd

I was the only boy from Birmingham - so I soon became classed as a local! Later on a crowd of evacuees came from Liverpool. When they arrived they were taken to the local primary school with their luggage and labels, where people came along and chose who they wanted as their boarders. I felt sorry for those who were left until last. We had two at the house where I was; there were so many Liverpool evacuees the school couldn't cope with them and us, so we as locals attended in the morning, and the children from Liverpool went in the afternoon.

But that situation didn't last long, as many returned home quite soon. Most of the new influx were Catholic, which created a problem as there was no Catholic Church in Builth Wells. So arrangements were made to hold Mass, confessions, etc. in a room over a temperance hotel in the High Street.

I remember one year planting potatoes (and later picking them), on the side of Garth Hill - a small hill just outside the town. Most of the available women and children were there. We also helped plant and pick potatoes at Samuel's farm on the Brecon Road.

The only real reminder of the war was one night when a German bomber crashed into a hill which we could see from the back window of the house - and the ensuing fire. The following day we hung around the local police station, in the hope of seeing the German crew, when they were taken to the railway station - to a prisoner of war camp.

When I was 9 years old I had a paper round at the little newsagents down the bottom end of town. Part of my job was to meet the early morning mail train and collect the daily papers to take to the shop, where they were sorted out for my first morning round before going to school. I did another round, either at lunchtime or after school. At times I helped out round the shop. I enjoyed this part of the job because I was able to handle the books and comics and even read them sometimes.

Some time later I left the little newsagents and went to W.H. Smiths, where again I did a paper round. This time, after meeting the train to collect the papers, I had to deliver some on the way back to the shop. I also had to meet the evening mail train to collect the evening papers from South Wales and deliver them.

As children we spent a lot of time up Garth Hill playing among the trees and long ferns. On the way back we would stop at Rowland's farm to watch the milking and have a drink of milk straight from the cow, something you would not be allowed to do now.

It was quite a short walk to Garth Hill from Tanhouse, across three fields to the bottom of the hill. A housing estate now occupies one of the fields - the one on which we used

Land Army girls operating a sheaf binder

THE MINISTRY OF FOOD
announce the opening of a

FOOD ADVICE SERVICE

AT

3, BRIDGE STREET
BUILTH WELLS

Open daily 10 - 5

for free recipes and advice on your food and cookery problems — commencing on **MAY 10th**

ALPHA HALL
BUILTH

WARTIME COOKERY DEMONSTRATIONS

will be given on

Friday, May 14th, at 6.30 p.m.
Wednesday, May 19th, at 6.30 p.m.

Demonstrations will also be given in surrounding villages — watch for poster announcements

THE MINISTRY OF FOOD, LONDON, W1. FOOD FACTS No. 148.

to go sledging in the deep snow. Sometimes the snow was too deep for the children from outlaying farms to get to school, so the school would shut for the day. One winter the snow was so deep we were able to build igloos in the field.

Monday in Builth was market day. Farmers brought their wives in by pony and trap to do their shopping, much of it at the Market Hall, which was part of the building where the newsagents was (now the Wyeside Arts Centre). Another of my jobs was to clean up the Market Hall on Tuesday.

My parents came occasionally to visit, but it was kept a secret until a few hours before they were due to arrive. I suppose it was a little unsettling, but I soon settled down again after they had gone back. Even my elder brother came once, with a friend. Both of them were to die later in the Royal Air Force over Germany. My brother was only twenty-two years of age and was a sergeant rear gunner in a Lancaster bomber.

"Smartly now . . . Sick para-a-a-a-de —HALT!"

By the late summer of 1942 the bombing of Birmingham had greatly reduced and it was decided I could go home, for which I was glad, but with mixed feelings. Builth Wells had made a big impact on my life - so much so I later cycled down there with a friend when I was sixteen years of age. When I later married I brought my wife here on honeymoon, and we spent many happy holidays here.

Jim Davies

Childhood Memories

There would be the drone of an aircraft on a dark night, when you couldn't sleep. My parents would say it may be returning to Germany after a bombing raid on Liverpool or Swansea. There was always the strict attention to 'blackout'.

One day there was the surprise of tanks breaking through a hedge, crossing the river and leaving tracks on a neighbour's field. We would hear heavy guns firing on the hill nearby. The dog would be afraid of this, as he was of thunder. All such instances and many more besides persist by way of fragments of my memory of the war years. A child's memory is very fragile, and what was actually witnessed can be confused by what one hears subsequently. For years afterwards there was a debate as to the rights and wrongs of the military occupation of Epynt which necessitated the evacuation of the inhabitants.

We lived in a farm cottage out in the country. It seemed to me, even at that young age, that we country people were safer and better off than those in the town, and especially the cities. Of course, rationing applied to everyone, but we were fortunate in having a large vegetable garden and an orchard of apple and damson trees. We kept chickens and received milk and butter from the next farm. Above all, we were blessed with good neighbours – all of them.

Epynt sign

Ours was only a very small family. Many large families had a much harder time. I also learned that living conditions in Europe were far worse. Adult discussion of radio and newspaper reports described a grim situation. People in France, Poland, Russia and elsewhere suffered terribly.

Unlike the First World War, few men from the farms were required to serve in the Armed Forces. Even so, some did and a few others belonged to the Builth Home Guard. There were men from the 'War Ag', Land Girls and, later in the war, German prisoners around. With all the uniforms, drill trousers and overalls 'khaki' was quite a dominant colour of my youth. The Germans impressed me greatly with their strength and athleticism. They seemed to work very hard and they were often willing to teach you something interesting. All in all, it didn't seem much of a war to me!

Jim with his mother

I learned, much later, that one quite grown-up young man who used to drive by our house was in fact only fifteen. He had been given a special dispensation by the Ministry to consider himself one year older so that he could 'legally' drive a tractor on the public road. At one stage, he and another neighbour of the same age worked on newly ploughed land on the hill at Tycapel where potatoes had been planted by women from Talgarth. I came to learn that it was the war of twenty years before that mattered to us. My father had served in the Great War of 1914-18. His brother was killed in 1917, leaving a widow with two young children. Two memorial plaques, large and framed, hung on the kitchen wall, a framed portrait of Lord Kitchener was placed above the fireplace of the front room and a colour photograph of King George V was upstairs. The personal tragedy continued to cast a dark shadow of sadness, although it was rarely mentioned, at least not in my hearing. It would seem that it was this earlier conflict that was 'our war', and not what was happening in the present. Even so, at least three of my cousins were serving in the Forces and we were fearful for their safety.

Nevertheless, the wireless bulletins received close attention. The bombing of Swansea, Coventry and especially the London Blitz was talked about with neighbours regularly and for long after. Yet, amidst the constant worry there was a touching faith in Mr Churchill, and that he would see us through. Key phrases from his speeches were memorised and repeated so many times. In contrast, the sinister threats of William Joyce (Lord Haw-Haw) with his "Germany calling" were met with a nervous mixture of alarm and disdain. Yet his acid tones were also mimicked time and time again. Was it really only propaganda aimed to demoralise? I can recall one particular broadcast when Lord Haw-Haw revealed an intimate knowledge of the Elan Valley reservoirs, and of his detailed warning of the devastation to be wrought when the dams were breached.

'he Squander Bug

Perhaps, most important of all, was the role of the wireless in keeping spirits up and boosting morale. The singing and light entertainment was invaluable. What was essential was to remember to take the liquid batteries to Builth on a Monday so that they could be recharged. No-one wanted to be without their wireless. On a regular basis the immediate concern was for raising funds for the war effort. I noticed just how careful my parents were with their spending and not wasting anything. I'm sure I became more scared of the spectre of the 'Squander Bug' than anything Lord Haw-Haw had to say.

Our parish school in Llanddewi'r-cwm was closed early in the war. It was said that Mr R.V. Kingston supervised the carrying of desks and materials down to the school at Builth. At some time around the end of the war – whether before or after I cannot remember – we were issued with various items, including tins of cocoa powder. We were also encouraged to collect 'hips and haws' and other fruits. However, the playground chanting of somewhat irreverent verses about Hitler was not encouraged.

Builth Wells war memorial

Sometime in the summer of 1945 I attended a celebration party in Castle Road (my cousins lived there and I suppose I must have been invited). I am not sure whether this was on V.E. Day or not, but I did know that this was the end of the war. Everyone was very happy that day. Flags and bunting, tea and cakes were everywhere. The following years were to teach us children more about the significance of the war, not least by the annual services of remembrance, the names on the war memorial and the stained glass windows in the church.

Norcliffe Lloyd

A young boy's recollection of the war in Builth Wells

Norcliffe (R) with Bernard Allen

When war began I was just 6 years old. I have some recollections of my own experiences during the war time years in Builth Wells.

At 15.30 hrs on 22nd August 1942 a Halifax Bomber crash-landed at Gellicadwgan Farm due to engine failure, going through a hedge that took out the two front machine guns and coming to rest with the starboard wing up against a tree and the rear turret over the River Wye. News travelled fast, and there was great excitement; here I am 9 years old, off on my own to the crash site. "*The pilot noted that several small boys were running off with ammunition that had been thrown out of the bomber*". As stated in the newspaper cutting – I was one of the small boys. There was lots of debris scattered around. My eyes lit up, I found a belt of ammunition - big bullets - I heaved it on my shoulder. I walked through a large hole in the hedge, probably caused by the plane crash-landing, heading for home. Alas, I hadn't got very far when I was relieved of my prize by a policeman and sent home.

The Groe was covered in tents belonging to the Americans and Canadians, months and months ahead of D-Day. The Americans were very good to us kids. I used to deliver papers to these troops, and also traded western comics for extra tea and sugar.

Halifax bomber

Mum was very pleased and thankful for these extras. I can also remember seeing a Lysander plane on what is now the showground. It was parked under a large tree, probably using it as camouflage – not to be seen from the air.

Builth was full up with evacuees. We used to have various gangs, from different areas of the town, and meet at the castle for crab apple fights. To me, as a child, rationing didn't seem too bad, just the lack of sweets! I also have some recollection of visiting some bomb craters – three in a row between Builth and Garth – made by German planes lightening their load on the way home, and of men in the T.A. being knocked up at two o'clock in the morning and loaded onto lorries.

Canadian soldiers and Jeep in the river at Builth

I remember watching Keith Powell, who was only little, driving round and round, all on his own in an American vehicle. He had been taught by the Americans. He fell out with the soldier in charge and drove the vehicle into the river right out to Builth Bridge and refused to drive it back. The Americans had to tow it back to dry land.

I can recall a prisoner of war camp up at Swingy Bridge made up of German and Italian troops. I remember looking through the gates, which were high mesh with a big padlock supplied by 'Bradleys of Builth'. I can also picture in my mind a face belonging to one of the prisoners, a German I think, sitting on one of the rocks up at "Hell Hole" one of the favourite places for the locals to swim. I would watch them, being too young to swim at that time. He would be there for about half an hour or so some days after finishing work on one of the farms. I was led to believe that he was a champion swimmer for Germany.

Llanafanfawr Home Guard

GRACE MCDONALD

MEMOIRS OF A TEENAGER IN THE WAR 1939 – 1942

Grace (centre) with Bernard Allen

I was lucky to have been born a girl. Most of our young men went to the Forces. Some never came back. I came back from Birmingham, where I had spent my usual summer holiday with an aunt and family, on the day before war was declared. I had to go to the Town Hall to be fitted with a gas mask, which, thank God, we never had to use.

Not realizing perhaps the full impact of war I couldn't help wondering what it was all about. Seeing sand bags being piled up in the streets, shutters and tapes on window glass made me think something really horrible was about to happen. We all listened to the news that Sunday morning and when Chamberlain said "We are at war with Germany" I thought – well, this is it! My father, with service in two wars, was thinking what he could do in this one. He was too old for regular service but joined, as it was then known, the L.D.V., having his former rank as sergeant. Also he became night watchman at the local factory which was in the Strand Hall at this time. Taking his work very seriously he made himself a leather truncheon to waylay intruders, and our little terrier dog went with him as night watchdog! The factory made small arms and at one time the breach blocks for Bren guns. So in its small way it became very important. Eventually he had a gun which he hung on a beam above his chair. This gun was provided by the Home Guard or 'Dad's Army' as we call them now. We also had a 'Dad's Railway', but more about that later.

It was a serious time but never dull in spite of rationing, blackout, clothes rationing and everything else. We were all busy, Mum cooking and trying to invent something out of nothing with our meagre allowance (people grumble today – why?). We had marvellous concoctions with dried egg and sweets made from dried milk and anything else we could get, dare I say it, from the black market. We had our own apple trees and a baked apple and baked potato made up for any other things we lacked. The bottom half of Garth Hill was ploughed up and we had a crop of potatoes like small footballs. Later, we had an allotment on the old workhouse grounds. The occupants were gone long since, but soon we acquired two deal tables from this old building. How we came by them is another story. We had taken in four "dusted" men, ex-miners, from South Wales who had come to dig air raid shelters on the old castle grounds. Luckily we never had to use them where we might easily have drowned as they filled with water.

Two of these gentlemen had lovely tenor voices, one having sung in the Carl Rosa Opera Company. I played the piano, so we had singing whenever possible. There was great activity at this time and because of the blackout restrictions we needed some form of blackout other than curtains. We lived in our underground kitchen but the sitting room where we had the piano was on the first floor. Soon four paying guests set about making blackout for the windows. The two singers, the Jones brothers, would make them for the bedrooms and Messrs Ward and Hickey decided to make shutters which turned out to be the more sensible idea.

There was always a friendly rivalry going on. The two singers held stage most nights and the other two were rather out of it. Their idea of the shutters was more sensible as when the Jones brothers made theirs they found we couldn't lift them to put them up. We really needed them as the A.R.P. men were on nightly vigil looking for any chink of light. It was necessary too as most nights during the raids on Liverpool we would hear the familiar drone of their engines and see flares dropping as they went overhead. If we went out at all we held our hand in front in case we bumped into anything and talked loudly so others could hear us coming. There was no T.V. in those days and if you were lucky you had a wireless, but I can remember not having even that, so we make our own amusement.

The pill-box at the western end of Builth

Listening to the news was an important event. Especially during the North Africa campaign. My father had a map on the wall from one of the newspapers, and would mark the Allies' advance. At night he taught my sister and me how to parry with the gun. We did not need to use this knowledge.

The music and singing went on for most of the war years. Solos liked 'Because', 'Macushla' and many others were always heard coming from Bank Villa. Any musician was made welcome and of these there were many with different stories to tell. We had a varied assortment of instruments left in our care while their owners were stationed here.

In retrospect I think that is why we never found life dull. Sharing was the key word, and helping others became our family's password. I had had an accordion from the age of 11 and played it regularly. When one of the visiting soldiers decided to leave his accordion, (120-button), I could play whenever I wanted to. I was sorry when he had to leave. Eddie, as he was called, was part of an act with his father on stage pre-war. The sequel to this was my mother, in Birmingham with her sister, passed by the Theatre Hippodrome and noticed the billboard outside. On it was a picture of Eddie and his father! So she left a message at the stage door and they went to see Eddie and his father. All visiting troops were made to feel at home. None of them were here for more than two or three weeks. News used to come how some were at a later date. Sometimes there was sad news, especially after D-Day. Another sad thing was there were a few killed on the range here before actually any conflict.

News would spread quickly and a lot would be saddened especially if the person was known to us. Hogmanay was a festivity we always kept because of my father. If someone could play Bezique or Monopoly we sat playing them or just music and singing until it was time for lights out or whatever. During this time I became very friendly with a girl and this friendship was to last fifty years, still does. We both had a love of music and both commenced our careers in the local Brecon and Radnor office. She eventually pursued a political career and I went in for business. However, our musical talents were much in demand during these war years. Her singing and my playing even took us to entertain on a Sunday evening at the local cinema with very raised eyebrows I'm sure! It was all in aid of a scheme to obtain new instruments. Then there were concerts for money for Wesley Rest Room for the troops and Toc H, all good causes. The list goes on. By now the South Wales miners had returned and we had Land Girls instead. Came our initiation into the art of knitting socks, balaclavas, scarves, etc. – never a quiet moment.

Some of the Builth land girls

It is during this time I became a member of 'God's Wonderful Railway' or, as I like to call it, 'Dad's Railway'. I had to have a good knowledge of geography, clerical work and Morse code! Yes, we had to transmit messages daily in Morse and also be able to take them down. Each station had its own signal and it was possible, when fully accomplished, to hear what was being transmitted from one station to the other. A lot of messages contained words relating to movement of wagons, etc. and the strange names took some getting used to.

Some extraordinary things happened too. One moonlight night one half of a goods train vanished to one station and the other half came to an abrupt halt with the guard wondering what had happened to Tom and the engine which had continued onwards. The first half eventually came back to investigate, where an irate guard stood waiting to tell the driver a thing or two. It was the shunter who got blamed in the end for not coupling up the wagons. An incident which happened which could have been very serious indeed for Builth and its inhabitants and something that was kept quiet at the time. We had enough talk of 'careless talk costs lives'. The thanks should go to our signalman on duty early morning when no traffic was expected, who noticed the sparks coming from the wheels of wagons coming from Builth Road. Some had ammunition aboard. Our signalman opened the crossing gates and changed lines to direct the runaway traffic into quarry sidings on another gradient thus avoiding a serious accident. The first years I worked in the passenger department but later on, when the girl who was there was taken into the A.T.S., I went down to the goods office.

Everything was so interesting but at least in this office I finished at half past five, whereas in the passenger office it was shift work and the last one finished at 8 pm. It was not very pleasant coming over the bridge in complete darkness especially in the winter months. A lot of army equipment was moved by goods train and at times there were wagons standing on one of the tracks with ammunition which I was always glad to see move out. Mondays were a trial. All small animals such as goats or calves had to have a sack around their rear. Some arrived without. Then began the trouble trying to find one suitable.

Train arriving at Builth Wells railway station

Most Mondays a lot of the farming fraternity arrived on midday trains. So, as it was a lot to try to cope with at the station I went down travelling on the footplate to book them up from Aberedw. What a change in transport over forty years! Every evening on the late shift in the passenger office we had a visitor come in to tell us his views on the weather and how the war was going. He was a vicar's son and worked for a firm of solicitors. He certainly could talk and the time went and sometimes he had to run for his train.

There were no church bells rung during the war but they would only sound as a sign of invasion so much as we missed them we preferred not to hear them.

The radio and Pathe Gazette at the pictures kept us in touch with the news. There were broadcasts from Churchill, who really kept us going in every sense of the word and on the black side we had Lord Haw-Haw, a traitor, giving his version of how things were. We had many different Regiments passing through - Czech, Canadian and American, black and white. The first chicken in a tin I ever had came from the Americans, who had parcels of things we had not seen here for years.

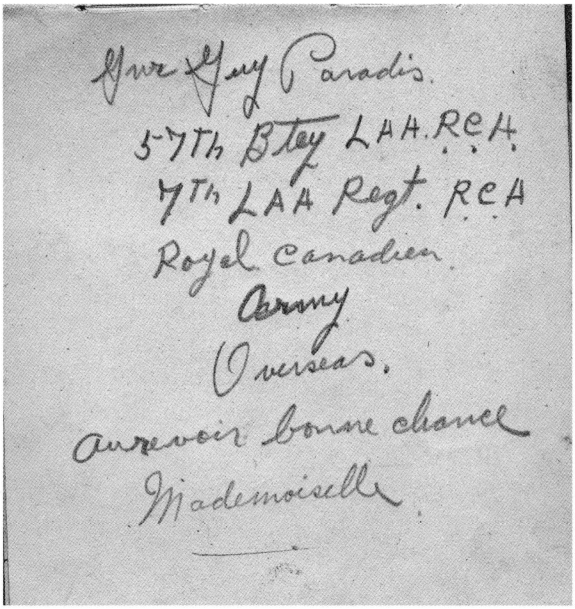

Wartime autograph book

Food rationing went on for a few years after the war, and food and furniture were on dockets. There wasn't any T.V., but our wireless became upgraded from a two battery wet and dry to an electric set. My work was in the 'reserved occupation' category and although my papers came for the W.R.A.F. I could not go. It was strange being the only girl except for our lady porter. Later we had a female porter on the 'deck', which was the loading bay for the goods trains.

The war in North Africa had progressed by now from El Alamein via Mersa Matruh and Sidi Barrani on to Tripoli by February 1942 and I was in my last teenage year. What an eventful time it had been, years I will not forget. Perhaps we do not have the freedom young people today experience, but at least we were at one in our outlook and a lasting memory. When I go to the Remembrance Service in November and hear the names of those I had known I say a silent prayer - thank you - I will remember.

Grace McDonald, December 1989

Dominica Jones

Neé Conti

Dominica (right)

On a bright Sunday morning my father had taken we 3 children to Mass in the Catholic Church in Llandrindod. Starting for home he realized that the car was low on petrol, and he pulled into Norton's Garage. Mr Hughes, the garage manager, spoke quietly to my father.

The time was just after 11 a.m. and he told Dad that our Prime Minster, Mr Chamberlain, had just spoken on radio to tell the country that our nation was at war! The date was the 3rd of September 1939.

My father drove very quickly in order to reach home, hoping that mother would not have heard the news on radio; however, she had, and was remembering the 1914-1918 war – not so very long ago. She was in tears. It was a very strange day. My father's shop (café etc.) was open every day, and later, in the evenings. He was uncertain as to whether to lock the door, etc. etc.

Builth seemed to change overnight, and, very quickly, everybody and everything seemed to get used to the strangeness of things. Adults and children all had to get used to a new way of life rapidly, such as blackout, rationing, coupons, shortage of petrol and men leaving for war!

Cartoon of life at Conti's Café by an American serviceman

As the first month or so passed, it seemed everyone became stoical. Our way of life would become very different. Soon, autumn would become winter, and children would have to be home earlier from playing, because of no street lighting. Shop windows were draped with long, black curtains so that no light shone into the street, alerting any enemy aircraft.
As time went by there was very little on display in some shops such as butchers, grocers and fishmongers. Foodstuffs were quickly used. Other goods such as clothing and shoes had to be bought by the coupon system, and these soon became scarce. Newspapers became thinner for want of paper and printing materials.

Cartoon of life at Conti's Café by an American serviceman (2)

Evacuees were chiefly from Liverpool and were children who were in danger in the large cities. They arrived by train with their teachers and found it very difficult to settle in Wales!

Some time later, fields at the end of town, alongside the River Irfon, were soon covered with tents, then later huts, to accommodate soldiers - American, Polish and, of course, British.

Very few cars (private) were to be seen, but other vehicles were to become commonplace. All sorts of motorised vehicles took troops up to the Welsh mountains - Epynt for example - for training before crossing the Channel into the war zones.

The Americans especially enjoyed our town when they were having leisure time, and soon everyone called them YANKS. They enjoyed the little time they had to spend in local 'pubs', etc. Children were given chewing gum and sweets, and soon caught on to the saying "Any gum chum?"

The surface of our roads, High Street for example, became badly pitted due to the excess traffic passing through. On one occasion an enormous tank, which was almost as tall as the flat over the shop, passed slowly by. It was a Churchill tank!!

The other occasion which presented the populous with another very large vehicle was the one which carried the fuselage of a Sunderland aeroplane. As it turned onto the bridge over the Wye it knocked into, and damaged, the canopy of the Lion Hotel!

And so the war moved on, until there was a great movement alongside the river – and parked beneath the beautiful trees up The Groe were vehicles of all kinds draped in camouflage netting. The soldiers – British and Americans – were en route to Dover; the start of the journey to sail across the Channel to start the assault on Nazi Europe!

The D-Day landings took place on June 6th 1944. On D-Day+6 – June 12th 1944 – Churchill crossed the Channel and went ashore in France.

German Surrender – May 7th 1945.

Before D-Day British, Polish and American troops trained and exercised on Epynt; after 2 or 3 weeks they left and others took their place. Rationing of food was stringent for businesses; e.g. butter, sugar and eggs and there was a severe quotient for dried fruit.

Facing north, from our home, late one night there was a red glow on the horizon to be seen. This was the bombing of Coventry. A young Builth girl trained as a nurse there, the hospital was totally destroyed and Cecilia arrived at home and later died of her injuries.

On June 12th 1944, as a student in college at Cardiff, I, and Peter Owen, also a student, were allowed home. We travelled by train into Builth station! We walked over the bridge to see street lamps and crowds of local people and soldiers dancing to music out in front of the Lion Hotel. Wonderful! I think it went on all night.

When British troops arrived in Builth, there were no camps but many soldiers. Properties were taken over to accommodate as many as possible until they had to use tents along the river alongside Swing Bridge.

Other accommodations were the Lion Hotel for senior ranks (colonels, etc.) and sergeants at the Queen's Head Hotel, on the corner of King's Head Lane.

Jazz band outside Conti's Café

Idwal Jones

Blaenbwch

At night cities like Swansea, to the south, were badly bombed and the sky was lit up with searchlights and glowed red due to the fires blazing there. On one occasion I was in the farmyard when a line of bombs was dropped across the valley. None exploded, so they were made safe by controlled explosions.

Inspecting a local bomb crater

Large numbers of British and later American soldier were based in Builth and trained on the nearby Epynt range. There were two camps and army vehicles and guns were parked along some of the roads (especially North Road) and under the trees on The Groe. At night guards would say "Halt! Who goes there? Friend or Foe?" to people walking around certain areas of the town. Blaenbwch was at the edge of the range and I remember the training that went on prior to D-Day; American tanks fired shells across the valley where I lived.

Ann Lane

They called me about 7.30 this morning (I lived in with the family on the farm). I sauntered down about ten to eight. Got the three cows in and milked one then had a cup of tea and went back to milk the other two. After that I had my breakfast. I then cleaned out the cow sheds, took the cows up to the orchard, took the sheep across the road, loosed the chickens, fed the pig, then cleaned a pathway between the two cowsheds. I then chopped a bit of firewood.

By then it was dinner time. After dinner I had a wash and a tidy up and then Trevor (the family's nine year old son) and I walked up to the shops to get the rations etc. When we came back I sat down for a bit then went for the sheep and brought them down to the building to put some Raddle on them (a coloured sheep marker). Then took them back, had my tea, got the cows in and milked them and, hey presto I had finished.

Nell Richards

Neé Ashburner

Land Army experiences in the Builth Wells Area

I had been working as a clerk in a co-op office in Leigh. It was boring and I wanted to join the W.A.A.F., but they were not taking on any more recruits.

I was seventeen and a half in 1941 and along came the opportunity to join the Land Army. My elder sister, Sally, and I filled in the forms and waited. I can't remember if there was an interview. We left Leigh to join the Land Army in June 1941.

I can remember travelling by train to Builth Station with a whole lot of girls from Lancashire and noticing in particular all the countryside and wondering what sort of place I was going to end up in. When the train stopped in Builth, a bus was waiting to take us to the hostel the other side of the bridge and we could see it from the bridge. There were 26 of us in one big dormitory; bunk beds stood next to small units about 2' wide consisting of a wardrobe and dressing table. I shared my bunk unit with Rene who became a friend. I slept on the top bunk.

Miss Edwards was the hostel's warden. We had a canteen and the food was served in a big dining room. We were given sandwiches every day to take to work. I cannot remember much about the food except that I ate so many baked beans I have hated them ever since! We had to wash our clothes in big baths, though I can't remember hanging them outside. You had to put your name on your clothes and petty theft was common. I didn't like the clothes we were supplied with, especially the corduroy trousers. I bought a better pair. I still have my Land Army issue shoes! They will never wear out. Later on the hostel closed, though I can't remember when or why, and we were found lodgings in the town. I lodged with Mrs McKay in King's Head Lane.

The 26 young women all arrived together and we were split into two groups of 13, one group working in Radnorshire and the other in Breconshire. I and a girl called Chris were the youngest. I can't remember anyone dropping out. I worked the Radnorshire group, although at some stage I did work in Breconshire. The depot was near Hundred House and the Fforest Farm and we started off from there each morning.

Tom Watkins was in charge of us Radnorshire girls and Ben Jones of the Breconshire girls. Tom Watkins was very good at his job. We worked five days a week, 8am - 5pm, and had the weekends off. I can't really remember how many holidays we had, probably a fortnight. We went home for Christmas.

I remember that the first job we were given was sorting potatoes on the different farms. It seemed to go on forever and in the end the potatoes were in a bad state. The main jobs we did were: ploughing, hoeing, threshing, cutting and binding (baling) the corn. Eventually I learned to drive a van and a Ford Fergy tractor. We didn't work with animals.

Land Army Workers.

ENTERTAINMENT PROVIDED IN THE TWO COUNTIES.

Mrs. Houston (organising secretary for the Women's Land Army in Brecon and Radnor) arranged for "Ensa" artistes to visit the five Women's Land Army Hostels in Brecon and Radnor. Mr. Lynn and partner (accordion and ukelele players) gave the last of the series of entertainments, which were enormously popular with the girls and their friends, at the Builth Wells Hostel on Friday evening, when Mrs. Gibson Watt (chairman of the Women's Land Army) warmly thanked the artistes and expressed the hope that they would be able to pay another visit to the hostels in both counties in the near future.

She presented 22 members of the W.L.A. housed at Builth Wells with good service badges.

Eddie Moore taught me to plough. At the first farm after my training, the farmer asked me which way was I going to plough the field. I told him "across". He said, "No, you are not. You always plough up and down a field". I never made that mistake again and I became very proficient at ploughing. I used to drive two of the men to work and then went on to work myself.

The social life was pretty good, especially as there was a constant turnover of British, Canadian and American servicemen training in the area and staying in the army camp in the Irfon Road, Pendre area. We frequented the pubs (I met Stuart in the Barley Mow), and attended dances, held weekly in the Drill Hall. Several women stayed after we finished: I can't remember when that was but I think it

WOMEN'S LAND ARMY PROFICIENCY CERTIFICATE.

THIS IS TO CERTIFY THAT

Miss. E. Ashburner. W.L.A. No. 85551.

HAS BEEN AWARDED A PROFICIENCY BADGE

IN Tractor Driving.

AND HAS GAINED DISTINCTION.

Date May 1944. Signed G. Denman.
on behalf of the Women's Land Army.

was after the war. Sally married Aubrey, who was involved with the WARAG; Clare married Howard Weale and I remember Chris moved to Talgarth.

I remember on one farm there were two farmers, one always wore a trilby and the other a bowler hat. They failed to give us so much as a cup of tea when we went to work there. One day, I was driving in the van and noticed them making their way to the market in Builth on foot. They expected me to give them a lift but I was so fed up of their meanness that I gave them a cheery wave and sped on my way! Thereafter, we were treated to a meal whenever we went there!

I also remember a lady farmer whose bulk was considerable – until one day she divested herself of coat after coat after coat until all that remained was a diminutive little figure.

WOMEN'S LAND ARMY (ENGLAND AND WALES).

RELEASE CERTIFICATE.

The Women's Land Army for England and Wales acknowledges with appreciation the services given by

Miss E. Ashburner W.L.A. 85551.

who has been an enrolled member for the period from

June 16th 1942 to February 28th 1946

and has this day been granted a willing release.

Date March 7th 1946. Lilian E. Houston
COUNTY SECRETARY, WOMEN'S LAND ARMY.

KAY BURNS AND MAY THOMAS

MEMORIES OF THE 'KINO' CINEMA, BUILTH WELLS

Kay Burns (second left) May Thomas (right)

Kay engaged as a cashier in 1945, with responsibility for taking bookings in the daytime, working in the box office each night and also selling sweets and chocolate in the kiosk. Every packet of sweets, chocolates, nuts, etc. was counted and had to be accounted for; any discrepancies had to be paid for by whoever was selling.

May Thomas (now Owen) started at the 'Kino' in 1940. The staff wore a uniform – the same colour overalls. When soldiers were stationed in the town the cinema was packed every night, with queues stretching down to Castle Street. Quite often there were 350 people in. Chairs were put down the aisles, and people sat on window sills and in every available space. There were no central steps, only a gradual slope.

Foreign soldiers sat through all the films even though they couldn't speak English. Many didn't understand the currency and would hold out a handful of money for the cashier to take what she wanted.

Smoking was allowed and there were ashtrays on the back of every seat. The ashtrays had to be emptied and checked for smouldering cigarette ends. During the war years there was an auxiliary fireman on duty every night. One – Mr Spacey – was a regular twice-a-week patron and would see the film whilst on fire duty and go on the following night to see the same film with his wife.

Kino Cinema and Market Hall

The building was heated by coke-fired heating. This is where the cinema cat slept; she was permanently covered in coke dust but was a good ratter, especially after a flood when rats were often seen running over the feet of patrons in the front rows – known as the 'chicken run'. The cinema was lit by gaslight. Films were collected each week from Cardiff. Stills were displayed on a board on the left-hand side of the main door.

Mr Taylor was a very strict but fair boss and expected staff to do a good job. The atmosphere was always a happy one and everyone got on well together. May received 12 shillings and sixpence per week.

July 10th 1995

JACK AND MURIEL BUFTON

THE AIR WAR COMES TO BUILTH WELLS DISTRICT

Junkers 88

Jack and Muriel Bufton awoke early on the morning of 27th April 1942 to much kerfuffle outside the remote farmhouse where they lived near Hundred House. 'Whatever is going on?' they wondered, seeing policemen and soldiers in uniform trampling across the fields outside the window.

Everything soon became clear. A German aircraft, a JU88, had been shot down during the night and the police and soldiers were searching for the wreck and for possible survivors, as at least one parachute had been seen by the Beaufighter from 255 Squadron that had shot down the enemy plane. The presence of so many friendly forces dispelled any fears she may have had. The wreckage of the German bomber was soon located on nearby Gwaun Ceste hill. The aircraft had crashed in flames but two of the four occupants had managed to escape by parachute, and were soon rounded up. They were the observer Walter Kreinenbrock and radio operator Paul Kochen. As we heard earlier it seems that one of the airmen attempted to surrender to a member of the Home Guard, but had to await arrest by the local constabulary when the Home Guard trooper fled in terror, leaving behind his girlfriend! The pilot oberleutnant Gunther Brixius and gunner Adolf Liebig were killed in the crash. Their bodies were recovered to the farmhouse, the rescuers unceremoniously bringing them down in wheelbarrows. This undignified mode of transport was in fact the most suitable as the track to the crash site was very rough and some distance from the house.

It later became clear that the dead airmen had served their country with great courage, as both were holders of the Iron Cross, one of Germany's highest awards for gallantry and one of these was recovered. Wedding rings engraved inside with the names of the deceased were also found. The airmen were initially interred at nearby Glascwm church but subsequently re-buried at the German War Cemetery at Cannock Chase. Ironically the pilot of the British PIC 4 Beaufighter, F/O Hugh Graham Stanhope Wyrill, D.F.C., was killed by German bombing in North Africa in November the same year.

Memorial at crash site

The crash site is still visited by both British and German citizens and a small plaque marks the spot. Efforts have been made to return the Iron Cross to the relatives of the owner. It seems the effects of war still have profound repercussions on survivors on both sides.

NEWBRIDGE-ON-WYE SCHOOL

THE EXPERIENCE OF WORLD WAR 2

(This information was collected by P.A. Jones, who was employed by UWIST at the Llysdinam FC)

Three days before the children were due to return to school in September 1939, Germany invaded Poland and two days later, on 3 September, World War Two began. Term therefore started a week late, by which time several evacuees had already arrived in Newbridge.

Prisoner of war camp at Newbridge-on-Wye

"Among the evacuees who came to Breconshire was my mother, my two-year old sister and myself, an ailing three-month-old baby. Along with thousands of others, my mother was ordered to join those assembling at London's Paddington Station late one night in 1940, during the height of the London Blitz. We were put onto a train not knowing where it was headed, with bombs falling all around, eventually arriving in Swansea while that city too was in the middle of a night bombing raid. After what seemed like hours of sheer terror for my mother, we boarded a train crowded with other evacuees, and headed for mid-Wales. Some evacuees disembarked at each stop along the route; we were taken off the train at Garth Station, with several others, and driven by lorry to Troedrhiwdalar Chapel, Llanafan. There, among the cottagers and farmers who had gathered to welcome us and take us into the warmth and comfort of their homes, we were enveloped by the diminutive Ophelia Jones and taken to wait out the war in the tiny cottage where she lived with her husband, parents, and two sons. This part of Wales has remained a haven for us ever since."

Newbridge-on-Wye was to host a large number of evacuees, the majority of whom were from industrial Bootle, a target area for bombing raids with its docks and proximity to

Liverpool. Children also arrived from London, Birmingham, Coventry, Luton, Birkenhead, Cardiff and Swansea.

While the war raged in Europe and cities all around Britain were devastated by bombs, the village calmly carried on as usual. On 17 October 1939 the Great Horse Fair was once more celebrated and the schoolchildren given the day off as a holiday.

Education authorities wondered how they could help the war effort. The Newbridge managers rejected the idea of turning part of the small playing field into a vegetable garden, due to its small size, but agreed to sell locally the produce from the school garden. Any surplus would go to the L.E.A., which would be asked to supply the necessary tools, seeds, manure, etc. This was part of a general "Grow More Food" campaign established by the Ministry of Agriculture and Fisheries in 1940 for which Sir Charles Venables-Llewelyn donated land for allotments to be worked by men from the village.

Bob Mason and Maureen Mason (now Dobins)

The teaching profession had always attracted numerous female teachers but many more were needed at this time because so many men had enlisted in the Forces. Most training colleges were located in cities and therefore vulnerable to German air attack and so student teachers did part of their training in smaller rural schools, such as Newbridge-on-Wye School. There had been the occasional student teacher at Newbridge previously but, in November 1939, eight student teachers from Cheltenham College visited the school for a week to observe teaching methods. In May 1940 six more student teachers came for one month to do some teaching practice, with another eight arriving in October 1940.

To help meet the need for teachers, a training college, Coleg Llandrindod, was opened in Llandrindod Wells during the war in the former 'Ye Wells Hotel'. It continued for a further decade after the war, before becoming a School for the Deaf and finally the Radnorshire College of Further Education (now Coleg Powys).

As the war raged on, concern was expressed for the children's safety in the event of an air raid or warning of one. The headmaster suggested plans for the distribution of children to houses neighbouring the school, and arranged to have a rehearsal. By September 1940 all the school windows had been covered with anti-splinter materials "as a protection against bomb blast." By October 1941 the school had received a supply of gas masks for the children and the headmaster instructed any children who had damaged masks to take them to the police station for repair or renewal. A gas mask drill was held at the school.

The villagers were likewise preparing for the worst. A gang from South Wales dug a tank trap filled with barbed wire across the main road through the village, near Alford's Bakery and Grocery, and pits were dug on the tips of the highest hills. Rhayader Rural District Council offered to provide sand to extinguish incendiary bombs free of charge to any Newbridge householder who required it.

Lancaster bomber over Builth Wells

The nearest the war came to Newbridge, in fact, was the jettisoning of some bombs over the village's Aberithon Bog by German planes on their way back from an air attack on Liverpool. It was also whispered knowledge that the Royal Air Force had used the Elan Valley Dams to practise dummy bomb drops in preparation for the raids on the Mohne Dams in Germany, immortalised in the film "The Dam Busters." The main object for the Lancaster bombers and their pilots, apparently, was to practise getting into the Elan Valley, fly along the dams and then escape over the mountains, as the terrain around the Mohne Dams was very similar.

Early in the war a scheme was developed to collect scrap iron which was desperately needed for making weapons, etc., and a lorry from Llandrindod Wells arrived once a fortnight to pick up any items not needed by the villagers. "War Weapons Week" held in April 1941 highlighted the need, and "Warship Week" in March 1942 resulted in the parish "adopting" H.M.S. Sentinel. Then there was "Wings for Victory Week" in May

1943 to raise money for the Royal Air Force, with a target of £40,000 set by the Rhayader Rural District Council and, finally, a "Welcome Home Fund" in July 1944.

The villagers were excited by the erection of a prisoner of war camp at the north end of the village, on some land owned by Major Gibson-Watt. The camp, which was commanded by Mr William Lewis of Cross Roads Cottage, housed some 60 prisoners. The first group of prisoners were Italians, who were sent out in gangs to carry out drainage work and other tasks on farms in the area. One farmer remembered, "They could make beautiful rings out of old threepenny bits, and cigarette lighters from all sorts of scraps, such as sardine tins. And when they were out draining, they'd catch frogs and sparrows and fry them." Another inhabitant recalled some of the Italians pretending to be "a leetle seek" to avoid work, and then spending the day in Llandrindod Wells. The next were Germans who were driven by Mr Len Powell every day to work at Rhayader Quarry. He recalled that they were poorly fed and dressed and he would often stop at the shop en route to buy them a loaf of bread. The third and final group were Ukrainians who entertained the villagers with concerts of singing and dancing at the Reading Room.

Early in 1940 accommodation at the school for evacuated children and their teachers was becoming a problem. In January 1941 18 Bootle evacuees were admitted to the school, accompanied by Miss Pearson, a teacher from St. Mary's Church of England School in Bootle. The School Medical Officer inspected the children and he sanctioned a double ration of free milk for 10 of them and a single free ration for the remaining 8. At the time Mr Thomas noted that 58 evacuated children had attended the school so far, of whom 38 children were still in attendance.

One month later, in February 1941, another group of children arrived from Bootle, mostly Roman Catholics, with their teacher, Miss Walsh. By the end of February the number of children on the school registers totalled 151, and the school was seriously overcrowded. The Military Authority had by now requisitioned the village hall, known by the villagers as the Reading Room, and the Director of Education decided to arrange for it to be de-requisitioned so that it could be used for educational purposes. The Reading Room was then taken over by the school and was visited by the Bootle School Medical Health Officer, along with the Bootle Director of Education, Canon Mason, and the Chairman of the Bootle L.E.A., Monsignor O'Brien. By the beginning of April the number of evacuees from Bootle totalled 56, with 4 from London and 1 from Birkenhead, plus another teacher, Miss O'Connor.

In April 1941 the managers discussed the question of school holidays and agreed that "under present conditions they should not be for longer than ten days at a time, and should be granted whenever the children's help would be most valuable on the farms, for harvest work, potato lifting, etc., and that the exact dates would always be subject to revision at very short notice." That summer the holidays were split up as follows: one week and one day from 11 July to 22 July for the hay harvest, three weeks in August for the corn harvest, and one week at the end of September to coincide with the lifting of potatoes. This pattern was maintained throughout the war.

Lumber Jills marching through Newbridge-on-Wye

It was not considered necessary to open the school during the holidays for the evacuee children, but the Reading Room was available at the discretion of Mr Thomas and Miss Walsh in consultation with the Vicar. One of the Bootle teachers remained at the school to organise walks and games during the holidays, with other teachers assisting on a purely voluntary basis.

By the end of March 1942 several Bootle evacuees had returned home, although 35 still remained at the school. These were supplemented by 12 children from Litherland, another Liverpool suburb, 12 from other parts of the country and 86 children from Breconshire and Radnorshire, making a total of 146 children sharing the school, the Reading Room and Llanyre Church Hall. The numbers were swollen by 8 teaching staff: 4 from Newbridge School, 3 from Bootle and a certificated assistant from Litherland.

The summer holidays of 1942 were again re-arranged to allow the children to help with the hay, corn and potato harvests and, in between times, the children were taken on expeditions to pick foxglove leaves, rose hips and blackberries, the latter being used for school dinners. The bombing raids on Britain lessened and, after the summer holidays, more of the Bootle evacuees returned home. Llanyre Church Hall was no longer needed as a classroom. One evacuee left prematurely. "James White, a Bootle evacuee, left his billet on Saturday morning and returned to Bootle. Police enquiry showed that he arrived at his home safely."

Mr Thomas, who suffered from occasional bouts of malaria, sustained serious injuries in September 1943. As Captain of the Newbridge Home Guard he assisted in the training of new recruits. One day, working in a pit near the Pistyll Farmhouse by Dol-y-Fan Hill, he was teaching a youth how to throw a hand grenade. The boy pulled the pin prematurely and was killed in the subsequent explosion. Mr Thomas was severely injured – "The bottom of his stomach was blown off," was one lurid description – and it was four months before he was well enough to return to Newbridge School. His injuries did not prevent him from resuming his duties. At the end of March 1944 he wrote, "I have been given leave of absence to take a battle platoon of Home Guards to the East Coast for a week's training."

Newbridge-on-Wye Home Guard

In the summer of 1943 9 more evacuees returned home and by June 1944 the mass evacuation scheme had ended. That summer London suffered a new kind of bombing attack from the V1 Flying Bombs and so evacuees returned home on 29 November 1944. The whole scheme had been enormously successful: it had saved the lives of thousands of children and had made many new friendships.

In April 1944 it no longer became necessary for the girls to travel to Rhayader for their cookery classes. Miss S. Price was hired as a domestic science and needlework teacher, conducting classes at Newbridge School on Mondays and Tuesdays and in Rhayader for the rest of the week. Both the cookery and the needlework classes were held in the Reading Room.

As the school gradually returned to normal, the classes were re-grouped. When Mr Mathias left in July 1944 to take up a post in Herefordshire the managers received only one application for the advertised position, and that was from a Miss Jones who was not willing to accept the offered appointment following her interview. Eventually Miss Gwenllian Pugh of Llandegley, a certificated and college-trained teacher, took up the position, on 1 October 1945.

In April 1945 the number of pupils on the books totalled 88 and they were organised as follows:

Infants:	Miss Lewis	26
Stds. I, II, III:	Miss Jones (later Miss Pugh)	23
Stds. IV, V:	Miss Richards	19
Stds. VI, VII:	Mr Thomas	20

At this time Mr Thomas was inexplicably sent four small hand bells, two rattles and one stirrup pump. "I have no use for these but I imagine they will give great joy to the boys, particularly the stirrup pump." Obviously conditions were more relaxed because, in May 1945, the war ended in Europe with the unconditional surrender of the German Army. During the children's summer holidays Japan surrendered and the Second World War was over.

BUILTH JUNIOR SCHOOL LOG

September 1st 1939
The Crisis: Instructions received from the Director of Education that members of the staff should return to duty immediately and stand by in case of emergency till Tuesday morning. School closure till further notice. Six shifts of four hours duration each were arranged. Members of the mixed and Infants Dept's. took their turn in pairs, and Mr D.E. Evans BSc, the County School assistant and Mr William Vest, the school cleaner offered their services to complete the number. Night duty was done by these together with Mr R.V. Kingston and self. Evacuated children were expected at any time. Mr Rice performed the necessary duty at the telephone at night (Bradleys). It is a pleasure to record one's appreciation of the faithfulness and willingness of the above mentioned during these days of the Crisis.
September 5th:
(Tuesday): The evacuated mothers and their children arrived in the afternoon. They were fed and billeted during the rest of the day. The School was closed at 10.15 pm billets had been found for all the evacuees from Liverpool etc.

Evacuees arriving at Builth

August 2nd 1940
School closed for mid-summer vacation till Monday September 9th 1940. During the vacation the school is to be protected from danger against air raids. All glass will be covered by either Tentest or Net (adhesive).

September 8th:
School commandeered by The Military - the 5th company Inniskillen Dragoon Guards.
September 15th:
The guards evacuated the school today.
September 16th-21st:
School closed for this week again to be disinfected and for A.R.P. purposes.
September 23rd:
School reopened following seven weeks closure (normal Summer Vacation was 5 weeks).
October 30th:
Six A.R.P. wardens examined and readjusted the school-children's masks this afternoon.

January 11th 1941
I. Walters Esq. visited the school pm. During his visit it was reported that the east end of the garden shed was ablaze which had been set afire by a burning adjoining shed in Mr A.P. Morgan's garden. The fires were extinguished by Mr Kingston, half a dozen boys, some civilians and soldiers.
February 19th:
Mr R.V. Kingston left school at 2.30pm to observe an A.R.P. demonstration and to practice exercises in extinguishing incendiary bombs. Mr Kingston is a member of the A.R.P.

Builth Primary School

March 31st:
Builth Wells War Weapons week to be held this week; commencing today, noon, with an inaugural ceremony in the Smithfield [Market]. Half holiday was granted to the children to celebrate the occasion.

May 11th:
(Sunday) School used for the reception of one hundred and seventy one (171) pupils from Merseyside. The numbers are as follows:

Litherland Boys Central: (age 11+)	21
Litherland Girls Central: (age 11+)	30
English Martyrs Roman Catholic : (ages 5-13)	40
St Elizabeth Roman Catholic: (ages 5-13)	21
St Phillips Church of England: (ages 5-11)	23
Bootle (4 Schools) Roman Catholic: (ages 5- 11)	20
Litherland Council: (ages 7-11)	16

May 12th-20th:
School closure: the week (May 12th - 16th) will be granted by the L.E.A. (Local Education Authority) for potato planting and a holiday on Monday May 19th for the Annual Builth Wells Children's Fair.

May 17th 1941
The Director phoned a message stating that the daily dual system of education was to be introduced on Tuesday May 20th. Hence:
1. All Builth Wells pupils will attend [School] from 9am to 12.45pm
2. All Merseyside pupils will attend [School] from 1.15pm to 4.45pm

May 23rd:
(Noon) School closure to celebrate Empire Day. During the morning lessons were given based on the Empire, and the importance of safeguarding it against the Forces of Evil and Injustice.
June 13th:
Lady Delia Llewelyn called to give information re the collection and drying of herbs (medicinal).
August 8th:
Builth Mixed School closed for summer vacation. All schools will reopen on Monday 1st September.
September 19th:
School closed for a fortnight for potato harvest.

P.B. Abery with grandsons

September 20th:
Saturday: Instructions received from the Director of Education cancelling the holiday for potato harvest as the potatoes are not yet fit. The crops were inspected today by a government expert. Announcements were sent to all the churches of Builth Wells cancelling the holiday for the present. Three teachers who had gone away were recalled by wire.
September 26th:
The postponed fortnight commences from today (Friday).

March 25th 1942
Warship Week. To celebrate Warship Week all the children were taken to the cinema. Every child purchased at least 3 penny stamps.
October 29th:
All gas masks in both departments were examined today by Mr Kingston and Mr Spoonley A.R.P. Wardens. Damaged masks were repaired. The children were given mask drill in every class.

May 4th 1943
Tuesday: This week is Wings for Victory Week for Builth Wells. The target set for this department is £500.
May 5th:
With special permission of the Director, all classes left at 2 o'clock for the Wings for Victory sports, held in the County School Field.
May 7th:
Friday: The National Savings Wings for Victory Campaign - the savings this week from Tuesday to Friday amount to £520.17.6. This campaign ends on Monday next. Total for the town and district this morning was £31,500. Target £40,000.
May 10th:
This department passed the target in the Wings for Victory Campaign. The total amount collected was £540.
May 11th:
Today we commenced the Salvage Drive which is taking place throughout the country for a fortnight.
May 25th:
Five tons fifty three pounds was the total weight of salvage collected by both dept's and the Evacuee School for the county drive during the last fortnight.
July 30th:
Miss E.M. Davies and Miss G.A. Jones granted permission by the director to absent themselves from duty this morning to travel for their holidays at an early hour, to avoid war congestion on railways.
October 30th:
Miss G. A. Jones absent this afternoon - travelling in daylight to avoid the blackout.
November 15th:
Under the auspices of the Agricultural Committee a set of four films on agriculture was shown this afternoon by the operator of the Ministry of Information. The 'show' was intended for farmers of Builth and District and the older children of the school. Only about half a dozen adults were present together with the senior department and the top class.

January 13th 1944
2pm. The whole department left the school for the Castle Cinema to attend a film show of 'Bambi', specially arranged for the local schools. This was the District Council's reward to the schools for the great effort in salvage collection this year.
May 18th:
Salute the Soldier Week's Campaign: to give the children an opportunity of celebrating this National Savings effort, sports were held on the County School playing field - the children with great enthusiasm left at 2pm under the charge of the staff. It was a delightful event.
May 19th:
The target for Salute the Soldier in this school was £500. The result was £1,051.10.0.

July 12th:
The time-table was rearranged this afternoon according to the Director's instructions. The afternoon session was opened at 1pm and closed at 3.30pm. This was done in order to prepare the building as a reception place for two hundred and fifty children (evacuees) from London, due to another Blitz (pilotless planes). Arrived here at 7pm. School open till 11pm.
July 17th:
All the Litherland children from the Horeb vestry were merged into the Infants and Mixed Depts of this school today. The acting head Mr Byrne has been recalled to Liverpool. The only teacher left , Miss Leeson, is attached to Std. 1 to help Miss Morris who has 46 children on registers according to the Director's instructions, 70 London evacuees occupied Horeb vestry today. The cookery class in this centre, Builth Mixed School was sent home by bus to attend their local schools. The centre was used as a classroom for 30 of the London evacuees.

July 19th:
The Director of Education visited the school today to arrange full accommodation for the London evacuees. Another classroom is needed. The Director instructed the London teachers to arrange their children into four groups. One group will remain in Horeb vestry. Three groups will be removed from Horeb and the cookery centre into three classrooms in the County School next week.
September 8th:
On Roll: Builth Mixed - 253, Bootle - 17, Surrey - 98; Total 368
September 12th:
All domestic science lessons were cancelled this week again as Mrs Davies, domestic science supply teacher failed to find lodgings. Builth is overcrowded at present - evacuees.

March 28th 1945:
Horeb Evacuee School was finally closed today. Mrs Farthing and Miss Rook returned to Surrey. The remainder of the [Surrey evacuee] School will be merged into the Council School after the Easter vacation. (By this time the number of evacuees on the school roll was down from 100 to 16).

BUILTH WELLS HIGH SCHOOL

DR COLIN HUGHES

The effects of the war were brought home to the 124 Builth County School pupils by the appearance of evacuees in their midst. The school had been officially designated as a centre for receiving refugees from Birkenhead, but few evacuees were received at all, and the majority of those were from the Southeast of England. There were six evacuees in the first [school] term of the war years - five were from the Southeast and one from the Midlands. Of the twenty evacuees in the register in 1940-41, eleven were from the Southeast, four from other Welsh towns (Swansea and Newport), the origins of two were unrecorded and only three came from Birkenhead, the official evacuating area. Five evacuees were received in 1941-42, one only in 1942-43, and two only in each of the subsequent war years.

From the summer of 1939, pupils had filled sandbags. ... During 1940, all windows were covered with fabric netting and high brick walls were built around the school to serve as 'bomb blast walls'. In 1942, a room in the school was designated as an 'Up-graded First Aid Point' with equipment to be used only 'in the event of Builth being bombed'.

The headmaster agreed to amend the timetable so that the school could be cleaned during the hours when there were no lighting restrictions. As a result, pupils complained of 'groping our way to school in semi-darkness'. The arrangements for A.R.P. satisfied official requirements; those pupils who could reach home within five minutes could do so, some taking friends with them. About 80 pupils (out of a total of 163) could remain on the premises in the event of an air raid, protection against blast and splinters being afforded by the passages and stone stairway within the school building.

The Board of Education had requested that Local Education Authorities should encourage the setting up of Air Training Corps. Builth governors were in favour and, because of the low number of boys at Builth, a start was made in conjunction with Brecon Boys County School and a flight of the A.T.C. was established in the summer of 1941. Training was provided in Morse, navigation and aircraft spotting, and most of the boys aged 16 and over enrolled.

By the end of 1941 the arrangement with Brecon had broken down, so the Builth Corps formed a separate flight, No. 1569. A well-attended drill was held during lunch times and this gradually replaced games! A club room was acquired at the nearby bowling pavilion, as well as an aero-engine for practical purposes. Members of the flight also attended R.A.F. camp holidays and visited R.A.F. stations. The flight existed until 1945, by which time no fewer than 54 ex-school pupils (out of a total of 150) had joined the R.A.F. Some old boys, like pilot officer Ronald Turner and pilot officer D. Morgan Jones visited the school whilst on leave and addressed the school flight. Both of them were later killed during operations.

Considerable efforts were put into war work, and into saving for the war effort, by the pupils of the school. A fund was set up to purchase wool, to knit gloves and other comforts for the troops. Weekly subscriptions were paid into this fund. Later they were to help the Post Office to issue ration books. All girl pupils, from Form 3 upwards, received Red Cross voluntary workers' badges at the end of the war for their efforts.

A school National Savings group was started in January 1940, and £1000 was quickly saved by the pupils. In May 1941 a total of £737 was invested in 'War Weapons Week'.

Dig for Victory

Added impetus was later given by organising the savings on a House basis; each of the three Houses was set a target of £100, the cost of a machine gun; the target was surpassed, £350 being collected. In May 1942 £1400 was invested in 'Warship Week'; and in May 1943 a target of £2000 was set for 'Wings for Victory Week', the aim being for Builth District to collect £40000, which would have been sufficient to provide eight 'Typhoon' fighters. In 'Salute the Soldiers Week', May 1944, the school broke all previous records by investing £3000. In the 4 special 'Weeks' £6500 was invested, bringing the school total of War Savings to £15000.

Wings for Victory Campaign 1943

Builth County School had been waiting for forty years to acquire its own playing fields. They were ready at long last in September 1939. Unfortunately, they were not used for their intended purpose because the Board of Education had suggested that "Schools should assist in increasing the stock of home-grown food by the cultivation of land which would not otherwise be cultivated at all". So the school governors gave permission for two acres of the school playing field to be ploughed and planted for oats, as part of the 'Grow More Food' campaign! During 1941, inspired by the 'Dig for Victory' campaign Form IV boys cultivated more of the land for potatoes and vegetables, and the girls cleared it of stones. A fine crop of potatoes was produced, two tons of which were used by the school kitchen for providing school dinners, as well as crops of carrots, parsnips and turnips. From the education point of view, the teaching of gardening and rural biology received a considerable boost, and this was typical of the times.

Immediately war started Builth County School lost two masters. The maths master became a captain in the Royal Artillery, and was later promoted to major. The governors continually asked for his release, but the Board of Education refused to write to the War Office, claiming that sixth form education could continue without him (this was not so - in February 1943 Higher Certificate maths pupils had to be sent to Llandrindod County School for instruction). He eventually returned to the staff in July 1944.

The P.T. master became a sergeant instructor (and later company sergeant major) in the Artillery Physical Training Service. He remained in the forces throughout the war and the school was to suffer, like so many others, from a lack of P.T. instruction.

The science master joined the searchlight unit of the Royal Artillery, serving from October 1940 to January 1942; and the English and history master became a flight lieutenant in the R.A.F. serving from late 1941 until 1946. The retired woodwork master was recalled and temporary mistresses were appointed. This was quite general during the war. (N.B. There were only eight members of staff at the above school - four, as can be seen, joined up).

Builth Wells teachers and pupils

BUILTH WELLS COUNTY SCHOOL

The following is a list of Old Boys of Builth Wells County School serving in H.M. Forces, published in the copy of the school magazine published Easter, 1945.

Names printed in heavy type are of those who have given their lives for their Country.

NAME	SCHOOL YEARS	SERVICE
Thomas Davies	1910-15	Army
David Ernest Jones	1912-17	Army
John Charles Belmont Humphreys	1912-14	Army
William Stephen Lennard	1913-17	Navy
Leslie Harry Jones	1914-18	Army
Alexander Liberis	1914-18	Army
David Henry Wynston Richards	1914-18	R.A.F.
Alfred William Davies	1915-18	R.A.F.
William John Evan Lewis	1915-17	R.A.F.
Cyril Isaac Price	1915-17	Army
John Ensor Duggan	1916-20	R.A.F.
Percy Lewis	1916-18	R.A.F.
Ivor James Lewis	1916-18	Navy
Ernest Davies	1917-22	Army
Clifford Morris Deacon	1917-19	Army
Cyril Lowes Davies	1918-20	Army (Australian)
David John Phillips	1918-22	Navy
John Meredith Bevan	1919-23	Army
Leslie Wilfred Howells	1919-21	Army
John Elwyn Jones	1919-23	R.A.F.
Cenfyn Powell Richards	1919-22	Army
Harold James Bicknell	1920-25	R.A.F.
Albert Meredith	1920-22	Navy
Idris Morgan Price	1921-24	Navy
Ralph Jenkin Weatherly	1921-25	R.A.F.
George Vincent Davies	1923-26	Army
Frances George Pegg	1923-28	Army
Merrill Edison Price	1923-27	Army
Emrys Williams	1923-25	R.A.F.
Raymond Arnold Williams	1923-26	Army
Leonard Vivian Price	1924-28	Army
Arthur Edward Stanley Davies	1924-28	Army
Frederick Horace Hardwicke	1925-27	Army
William Albert Jeynes	1925-26	Army
David Morgan Price Jones	1925-31	R.A.F.
Thomas Harold Jones	1925-29	Army
Roderick David John Lewis	1925-28	Army
John Berwyn Price	1925-28	Army (P.O.W.)
David Gwyn Richards	1925-28	Army
James Kendrick Pugh, M.C.	1926-28	Army
Arthur Lloyd Ricketts	1926-29	R.A.F.
Harold David Taylor	1926-29	Navy
Arthur Lewis Davies	1927-30	Navy
Thomas Llewelyn Richards	1927-33	R.A.F.
Harold Davies	1928-32	Army
John Isaac Griffiths (Mentioned in Despatches)	1928-34	Navy
Arnold Gwynne Jones	1928-35	R.A.F.
Evan Price Lawrence	1928-35	R.A.F.
Gilbert William James Pugh	1928-34	Navy
Richard Anthony Sayce	1928-34	Army
Harry Trevor Wilkins	1928-34	Army
Walter Edward Abraham	1929-34	R.A.F.
Douglas Stephen Edmunds	1929-35	R.A.F.
Reginald John Hurford	1929-34	Army
Frederick John Pryce Joseph	1929-34	Army
William Aubrey Morris	1929-34	Army
David Douglas George Powell	1929-33	Army
David Willis	1929-32	Army
Kenneth Howell Bevan	1930-36	Army (P.O.W.)
Oliver Davies	1930-37	Army
Ronald Matthew Jones	1930-37	R.A.F.
John Leslie Newell	1930-32	Fleet Air Arm
David Elvet Price	1930-37	Army
Wilfred Raymond Pugh	1930-34	R.A.F.
Dennis Miles Sayce	1930-36	Army
Frank Thomas Wilding	1930-31	Army
William Guy Wilkins	1930-34	Army
Rowland Edgar Price Williams	1930-37	Army
Thomas Pryce Williams	1930-34	Army
Douglas Howell Bevan	1931-35	Army
Reginald Gwillim	1931-37	Army
Alwyne Thomas Harley	1931-38	Army
Herbert Charles Lloyd	1931-35	Army
Ivor Llewelyn William Powell	1931-36	Army
David Lloyd Prosser	1931-37	R.A.F.
Ronald Vincent Turner	1931-37	R.A.F.
John Kenneth Daft	1932-39	R.A.F.
Kenneth Ernest Jeffrey Evans	1932-38	R.A.F.
David Ellis Jones	1932-35	R.A.F.
Frederick Kenneth Lamacraft	1932-37	Navy (Merchant)
Evan Alun Morgan	1932-38	R.A.F.
John Rees Cecil Morgan	1932-38	Navy
Philip Lanwarne Morris	1932-36	Army (Australia)
Victor Caradog Newell	1932-36	R.A.F.
Thomas Elwyn Price	1932-36	R.A.F.
Glaslyn Roberts	1932-36	Navy
Thomas Edward Turner	1932-36	R.A.F.
Charles John Williams	1932-38	R.A.F.
Evan Ellis Williams	1932-36	Army
William Neville Williams	1932-37	Army
Dennis Idwal Davies	1933-37	Army
Sidney Lynn Davies	1933-39	Navy (Merchant)
Oswald Meredith Deans	1933-40	R.A.F.
Donald Pryce Jones	1933-39	Army
Edwin Philip Jones	1933-37	Army (African)
Thomas Henry Jones	1933-39	Navy
Hugh Thomas Morris	1933-37	Army
Thomas Stanley Pritchard	1933-39	R.A.F.
John Michael Colin Turner	1933-38	R.A.F.
Ronald Thomas Crimmings	1934-39	R.A.F.
John Rees Davies	1934-39	R.A.F.
Bertie Lewis James	1934-36	Army
David Vincent James (Missing, November 1944)	1934-40	R.A.F.

NAME	SCHOOL YEARS	SERVICE
Arthur James Morgan	1934-37	Navy
Leslie John Garfield Powell	1934-38	R.A.F.
Cecil Edward Price	1934-40	R.A.F.
David Griffith Price	1934-39	R.A.F.
Gerwyn Claude Tasker Price	1934-38	R.A.F.
Hubert Trevor Pugh	1934-36	R.A.F.
Robert Wynston Richards	1934-41	R.A.F.
William Stuart Richards	1934-38	R.A.F.
Robert Waddington Sayce	1934-40	R.A.F.
Reginald ThomasStanton	1934-37	Army
William John Williams	1934-38	Army
Colin Crawford	1935-39	R.A.F.
Brinley Morgan Evans	1935-37	R.A.F.
David Ernest Evans	1935-37	Army
Geoffrey James Hamer	1935-40	R.A.F.
Herbert Mostyn Jones	1935-39	R.A.F.
Wilfred John Price	1935-38	Navy
David Charles Rowlands	1935-41	Army
Edwin Ronald Button Stedman	1935-40	R.A.F.
Albert John Trevor Turford	1935-36	Army
Ernest Latham Parry Bevan	1936-38	Army
David John Owen Davies	1936-40	Army
Sidney Gwynfor Evans	1936-41	Army
Thomas Alwyn Jenkins	1936-40	R.A.F.
William Sidney Jones	1936-40	Navy
George Albert Thomas Melhuish	1936-40	Navy
John Owen	1936-41	Army
Frederick Charles Phillips	1936-38	Army
David Coville Price	1936-41	R.A.F.
Arthur Valere Richardson Price	1936-41	Army
David Rosslyn Powell Pugh	1936-42	R.A.F.
John Walter Weale	1936-42	Army
Brinley Trevor Breese	1937-41	Army
Hugh James Downs	1937-40	Army
Edward Vaughan Harper	1937-44	R.A.F.
Thomas Austin Jones	1937-42	Navy
Gwyn Hopkin Morgan	1937-44	R.A.F.
David Pritchard	1937-38	Navy
Lennard Morlais Davies	1938-42	Navy
Kenneth Jones	1938-43	Army
Benjamin Edmund Tarrant Pugh	1938-41	Army
Frederick Arthur, D.F.M.	1938-41	R.A.F.
Vincent Howell Bevan	1939-43	Navy
Jeffrey Royden Hibbert	1939-40	R.A.F.
Arthur Desmond Matthews	1939-43	Navy
Douglas Richard Powell	1939-42	Navy

Staff

W.G. Whiteman	(Major, R.A., September 1939 July 1944)
F.J. Anthony	(Flight Lieutenant, R.A.F.V.R., November 1941)
B. Reynolds	(Bombardier, R.A., October 1940 January 1942)
H.H. Jones	(C.S.M.I. in Army Physical Training Service, October 1939)
H.H. Lewis	(2nd Lieutenant, Royal Corps of Signals, July 1940 - July 1942)

FRANK EDGAR BOX

PILOT 240 SQUADRON, R.A.F.

"It's san fairy ann to me!"

Frank Box was a highly skilled engineer in Birmingham prior to the war. He had married a local girl whom he had courted by cycling to Builth Wells every weekend. He volunteered for the R.A.F. when war broke out and spent much of his pilot training in Canada flying the Anson Mk 2. During one particularly difficult flight he eagerly asked his instructor how he had done. "Today Box," the instructor replied "you would have made a bird airsick!" Undeterred he completed his training and was assigned to 240 Squadron flying Catalina seaplanes on reconnaissance and anti-submarine patrols over the North Sea and Atlantic.

In March 1942 the Squadron left for India and spent the rest of the war flying anti-submarine and anti-shipping patrols over the Bay of Bengal. Once, whilst returning from a reconnaissance mission, Frank came upon a Japanese submarine which he immediately attacked. Flying boats were slow moving and submarines were well defended with anti-aircraft guns so during the attack his aircraft took a lot of hits but disabled the submarine with bombs and guns. He limped back to base in his damaged plane and reported the incident to his superior, informing him that the Japanese submarine would be there in the morning due to the damage he had inflicted upon it. Noting the severe damage to the aircraft his commander commented "It had better be, Box, it had better be!" This was about the time the Squadron was converting to the newer Sunderland seaplanes.

Many pilots lost their nerve during combat missions and although their 'wings' could not be taken from them they were looked down upon by the hierarchy and given menial tasks to perform, and LMF added to their name – "Lack of Moral Fibre". Frank did sympathise with these unfortunate men, battle stress wasn't considered then. The Squadron disbanded in 1946 and Frank Box had to fly his plane back to Britain. This was accomplished in stages over several days but once he arrived back in "Blighty" he did bend his orders somewhat by flying directly to Builth and performing aerobatic stunts over the town; he even observed his wife hanging out washing in the garden, but although she was aware of the unusual behaviour of the flying boat overhead she never guessed it was her husband trying to tell her he had returned safely from the war. He spent the rest of his life in Builth Wells working as a painter and decorator.

T. HARRI JONES

ROYAL NAVY

ADAPTED FROM A LUCKY JONAH
DR. P.B. JONES

T.H. Jones - Harri to his family, left the sixth form at Builth Secondary School in June 1939. Like many of his generation Harri's outlook at this time was essentially pacifist and in October he set off for university. Harri began a relationship with fellow student Claire Jones and at the first opportunity brought her to Builth for the weekend, on the crossbar of his old bike, to meet his family.

He wrote that he found Builth changed. The flower beds on The Groe were now vegetable patches, evacuees were everywhere and the benches in The Groe were even more popular than usual with all seats taken by "9.0pm and the blackout much appreciated."

Soon after the German attack on Russia, Harri, with no family history of the sea or indeed the ability to swim, surprised his family by volunteering for the Royal Navy. He was sent to H.M.S. Ganges in Harwich for initial assessment, then to Gloucester for basic training and finally to H.M.S. Scotia in Ayr to become a telegraphist. By now his sister Brenda was in the W.R.A.F., another sister Myra was in the Land Army, whilst his father Llew, a veteran of the First World War, was put in charge of the Llanafan Home Guard.

Harri's first ship was the destroyer H.M.S. Airedale. However, to get to her he had to take the long dangerous passage via South Africa and back through the Suez Canal to Alexandria to avoid the Axis dominated Western Mediterranean. Whilst on a brief break at Alexandria in Egypt, he contracted influenza and missed his posting. The Airedale was attacked by Italian planes and then sunk by a U-boat with the loss of 44 lives. His family thought him lost. But Harri had been reassigned to H.M.S. Seaham, one of the escort destroyers that protected the Malta convoys on the passage to and from Africa. He spent most of the war on the Seaham. There were long periods of boredom at his telegraph keys just waiting to be attacked on what he termed "the lecherous and griefless sea."

'Whilst I repeated mechanically, meaninglessly,
"Get the bastards get the bastards", for once
En rapport with our gunners - I was trapped
In a box with dot-dash- dot - dash hammering
My head.'

A particular incident recalled was the loss of the merchant navy ship Snapdragon with the convoy captain aboard. When the rescue boats went to pick up the survivors another stick of bombs "carried them away." Harri, for once on deck, was visibly shaken from watching the incident and he went below and picked up the wrong glass from the mess table and downed a full glass of vinegar. With a straight face he said, "I think I'll have my rum ration next."

Harri wrote his first mature poetry during the long periods of 'ennui' between bursts of intensive enemy action. He also became the mess scribe for the many illiterate crew members, and once when he had to write up a court martial he made a conscious "botch" of it because he felt the verdict was unfair. His view was that in the "First World War educated men had died leading the uneducated into oblivion whilst in the Second World War the truly educated men were in the ranks and the officers were often idiots."

In July 1943 Sicily was invaded and Harri was involved in a key incident. The Seaham surprised an Italian submarine the Bronzo on the surface which they shelled despite it surrendering. Bits of bodies were everywhere – the wounded captain was summarily shot and charts recovered that enabled the main Italian naval base of Taranto to be taken with limited loss of life later in September. Harri's great war poem 'Lucky Jonah' in part commemorates this incident.

Harri with sister Brenda

In October 1943 the Seaham left Harri ashore in Algiers at H.M.S. Hannibal, whilst it went off to take part in the invasion on France. Harri's expertise at languages and communications was needed more as a shore based telegraphist. Soon he became bored of Egypt and shore life and asked for a transfer. He joined H.M.S. Westminster running the courier service to Norway – out of the frying pan into the freezer – narrowly missing being torpedoed on many occasions.

With war coming to an end Harri was transferred to H.M.S. Wildfire in Sheerness where as an educated rating he taught English, history and politics on one of the vocational courses set up to keep the soon to be demobbed servicemen happy whilst they waited to return to civilian life. Transferred to H.M.S. Collingwood in Hampshire he met his future wife Madeleine Scott who was also teaching. He began to look forward to seeing again the calmer seas at Aberystwyth, so in his demob suit, minus shirt collar and cufflinks, he took the train back to Wales to complete his degree.

Thomas Henry Jones, or T. Harri Jones as he became known, died in Australia in 1965. He became one of the most important Welsh poets of the 20th century.

Arthur William Mackintosh M.C.

(Bill Mac) Royal Artillery

"Bill Mac" was a local man, probably best remembered as the charismatic headmaster of Llanelwedd School between the years 1966 and 1985. Although a colourful, outgoing character he rarely spoke about his war years.

As a member of the Territorial Army he was called up as a lance bombadier but soon after went to OCTU and was posted to France in 1940 serving with the 51st Highland Division.

The majority of the Division were captured at St Valerie en Caux three weeks after the Dunkirk evacuation but Bill was one of the few who made it back to Britain. He then served with the 59th Medium Regiment, Royal Artillery, taking part in the D-Day landing into the Falaise Gap and Caen. During severe fighting around Eindhoven he was severely wounded and was awarded the Military Cross for supreme gallantry.

The citation states: *On 15th and 16th September 1944 this officer was a forward observation officer supporting an infantry brigade in the assault crossing the Junction Canal. By great initiative he got his carrier and wireless sets across the canal under heavy shell fire and established his observation post. For two days this observation post was under observation by the enemy and was subjected to direct shell and mortar fire and continuous small arms fire. The enemy made a series of counter attacks during which time Captain Mackintosh displayed great courage and beat off the attacks on the observation post. Despite the fact that the observation post was hit constantly and despite the many counter attacks, Captain Mackintosh maintained communications with his guns throughout and directed the fire of medium artillery. This was so effective as to cause great loss and damage to the enemy and contributed materially to the successful defence of the Junction Canal bridgehead.*

Due to the wounds he sustained during this battle Bill spent nine months in hospital, and afterwards was posted to Builth Wells as adjutant to the Fifth Field Regiment, Royal Artillery. Thereafter he was part of the occupation force in Germany and ended the war with the acting rank of major. William Mackintosh revisited Normandy many years later with his family but found the memories unbearably distressing. We know from his family that some of the worst experiences apart from Junction Canal happened at Thierry Harcourt, Falaise Gap, Fecamp and Honfleur. Bill Mac was indeed a hero.

FREDERICK EDWARD JOHN PROBERT

MERCHANT NAVY

Fred Probert was born in 1922 and lived at Upper Shop, Newbridge-on-Wye. He joined the Merchant Navy shortly after the outbreak of war. He was posted to the tanker "North Cornwall".

In early April 1940 the tanker docked at Narvik, Norway to take on supplies. At that time German naval vessels were lying in wait off the coast of Norway to attack British vessels when they sailed out of the shelter of Norwegian territorial waters.

Whilst "North Cornwall" was loading supplies Germany invaded Norway. German destroyers sailed into Narvik fjord and opened fire on a Norwegian training ship moored near "North Cornwall". The Norwegian ship caught fire and sank.

The German destroyer then sailed alongside "North Cornwall" and the sailors were forced to surrender. Everyone, including Fred Probert, was taken to a German supply ship standing nearby. This supply ship was sunk in the first British naval attack on Narvik. Thirty-two members of the "North Cornwall" crew got ashore in one boat. However, four of the crew of "North Cornwall", including Fred Probert, were separated from the rest.

The thirty-two sailors linked up with some other prisoners, who were survivors from the "Hardy" which had also been sunk by the Germans, and they escaped from their German guards, who were unsure as to whether the men were still prisoners as they were now on Norwegian soil. They were picked up some time later by one of H.M. ships and brought back to England.

Fred and his three fellow crew members were taken ashore in a separate boat and held prisoner in a school in Narvik which had been commandeered by the Germans.

The prisoners were poorly treated. Food was in short supply and rations consisted mostly of dog biscuits. About 16 days later, as the Germans were unable to find enough food for either themselves or the prisoners, all the prisoners were marched off towards the Swedish border. The column was at one point shelled by a French destroyer, which mistook them all for German troops.

On 2nd May 1940 Fred's parents received news that he was safe and well, although interned at Jorn in North Sweden, about 1 degree south of the Polar Circle. Fred was with 129 other internees, all accommodated in the Salvation Army hostel in the town. On 24th August Fred's parents were informed that the British Consul in Stockholm was arranging to have warm clothing sent to the internees for the winter months.On 6th September 1940 Fred was transferred to Halsingmo, Soderhamn, Sweden with the other internees, where they met sailors from "H.M.S. Hunter", which had also been sunk off Narvik. The internees worked on road making, provided by the Swedish Government, and were paid about 20 kroner for 24 hours work per week. The men were all provided with overcoats, warm underclothing, working clothes, dungarees, blouses and gum boots. Fred subsequently volunteered to help run the blockade to England and on 30th September 1941 was accepted as deck crew on the "M.S. Dicto".

Fred and friends in Sweden

On 21st March 1942 the "Order of the Day", issued by Sir George Binney to the masters, officers, crew and other volunteers aboard "M.S. Dicto", M.T. "Buccaneer", M.T. "Lind", M.T. "Rigmor", "S.S. Charente", "M.S. Lionel", "S.S. Skytteren", "M.T. B.P. Newton", "M.T. Storsten" and "S.S. Gudvang" read as follows: "Today at long last we are going to England determined, come what may, to render a staunch account of our voyage, as befits Norwegian and British seamen. Indeed we run a risk, but what of it? If we succeed these splendid ships will serve the Allied cause and with their cargoes we shall aid the task of war supplies.

To sink our ships and cargoes rather than to see them captured by the enemy is of course our duty, and on your behalf I have taken such measures as you would wish.

Should we encounter misfortune at sea, remember that in our homes and among our countrymen it will be said with simple truth that we have done our best for the honour and freedom of Norway and Britain; but I, for one, have never held with this blockade and look once more to our success, believing that before two days have passed your laughter will resound within a British port. So let us Merchant Seamen – 400 strong – shape a westerly course in good heart counting it an excellent privilege that we have been chosen by Providence to man these ships in the immortal cause of Freedom. God speed our ships upon this venture.

Long live King George. Long live King Haakon.

M.S. Dicto

Gothenburg 21/3/42

Signed: George Binney"

Fred
was discharged from "M.S. Dicto" on 14th September 1942. He flew back to England in a Blenheim bomber.

In March 1943 Fred was paid a "Special Operation Performance War Risk Regulation Bonus" of £64 15s 11d.

e Birmingham Mail 6·30

BATCHELORS' The Fashion House We have an Attractive Range of COSTUMES & COATS Style and Quality at Best Coupon Values 63 & 64 HIGH STREET BIRMINGHAM 4

THURSDAY, MAY 10, 1945 ONE PENNY

ANDS

TAL WAR IN FAR EAST

E U.S. FORCE TO LEAVE EUROPE

LIES TO POOL SHIPPING

ie whole Allied world ed to-day from its cings over victory in pe to the sober realisa- that the war against Japanese remains to be Commanders in the Far , says Reuter, promised vift conclusion to the ggle, once the Allies' th of material and -power is concentrated nst Japan.

ral Sir Claude Auchinleck, nder-in-Chief India, said: nd is sure and cannot be long if each one of us puts forth her full effort. We must not hat the Japanese are as great ce to our way of life as were zis."

enant-General Daniel Sultan, nder of American troops in ndia-Burma theatre, said a's industrial strength can rn its full productive force to

The King and Queen were given a tremendous reception during their victory tour of the East End of London yesterday.

Mystery of Missing Nazi Leaders

GOERING'S STORY OF QUARREL WITH HITLER

Mystery still surrounds the fate of the Nazi leaders.

CONSCRIPTION FOR SOME YEARS

TO RELIEVE LONG-SERVICE MEN

SUPER-FORTS' BLOW

400 SMASH JAPANESE NAVY AN ARMY FUEL STATIONS

VIAN'S CARRIERS IN ACTION AGAIN

There are indications that a sterner phase in th operations against Japan has already been entere upon. American Super-Fortresses have struck a one of the weak links in Japan's armour—aviatio fuel supplies—and the British Pacific Fleet ha delivered sharp new blows.

The strike by the Super-Fortresses was the bigge yet made in the Far East. Over 400 of these gia bombers to-day attacked oil storage stations.

The targets, cables Reuter's correspondent, included the Japanese Navy's No. 1 fuelling point—Tokuyama, which is located on Honshu, 48 miles south-west of Kure naval base on the Inland Sea.

The army's No. 1 fuelling point, Tokuyama synthetic fuel factory, lies so close beside the naval fuel station that the two objectives formed a single bombing target.

Bombs from Medium Level

The largest known oil storage unit in the Japanese homeland was another target. This is Oshima, a

PETROL RATIO

BASIC SUPPLY O MODEST SCALE

WITHIN 30 DAYS

The Prime Minister announced the House of Commons to-day t a modest basic ration of pet

Percy Owen Prynne

Royal Artillery & Royal Military Police

As told by Tony Prynne

Dad (Percy Prynne) served with the Royal Regiment of Artillery enlisting in January 1932 at Newport, Monmouthshire. In January 1935 he left the Army, coming to Builth Wells as an A.A. patrolman covering Builth Wells/Rhayader/Llanwytyd Wells. He was responsible for putting the A.A. boxes on 'Sugarloaf', Llanwyrtyd Wells, and one at Devil's Bridge and the A.A. Box near Builth Wells railway crossing. The patrolmen rode on bicycles in those days, so it was a long day. It was here he met my mother Doris Kitchen who worked in Llandrindod Wells, cycling to work some days and using the train from Builth Road on others. They married on Christmas Eve 1936.

As a Reserve, he was called up in 1939 and served in the Royal Artillery as a gunner and in September of that year was in France with the British Expeditionary Force where he saw a lot of action. I am told that his Battery shot down the first plane using anti-aircraft guns and I remember that in the cellar of his home (my grandfather's house) was a large swastika from the tail of a German plane.

My mother received a telegram stating that he had been reported missing at Dunkirk. Our home at this time was in the lower flat that is now Conti's Newsagent's shop. Three weeks later Dad turned up together with a group of other servicemen who were all held in custody as they had to be checked out due to fear that they may be fifth columnists. He had escaped to Britain after finding a beached boat/barque, and refloating it. Together with approximately 20 other abandoned servicemen he crossed the Channel to England.

He was transferred to Corps of Military Police in Motor Transport with the rank of lance corporal and served in B.N.A.F. landing in Sicily in July 1943, crossing into Italy September of that year. On 2nd December 1943 he survived a huge explosion in Bari, Italy when an ammunition ship blew up killing and injuring many and causing considerable damage.

Dad met several other servicemen from the Builth Wells area whilst in Italy, including Frank Metcalfe whom he knew well. Prior to the war Percy Prynne had been a time-served motor mechanic and he returned to this trade after the war working with Mr Offa and Frank Tong at H.T. Price garage in Smithfield Road then accepting a post as drains officer with the "War Ag" in North Breconshire. In 1951 he purchased a garage in Llangammach Wells.

Bernard Teideman

Royal Welch Fusiliers & Somerset Light Infantry Band

I joined the Army on November 16th 1944 and started my service at Blackdown Barracks, not far from Aldershot, and after 10 weeks training was posted to Dering Lines, Brecon for another 10 weeks training. I then moved to Crickhowell near Abergavenny. We finished our training near Mynydd Du. On Good Friday, 1945 I was taken ill with appendicitis and 16 days later was on my way to Garth House near Builth Wells for recuperation. I asked Matron how far it was to Newbridge-on-Wye as I had an aunt living there, a Mrs Jones at Trefelyn.

On the Wednesday I was given permission to go to Newbridge-on-Wye on the bus. I asked the driver to let me know when we got to Newbridge. The driver told me that the elderly man sitting behind me knew everyone in Newbridge, so I asked him for Mrs Jones of Trefelyn.

He showed me the turning and said it was just up the road, in fact it was quite a walk. I passed a farm where I asked a young lady if it was much further to Trefelyn, she said it was not much further. I was welcomed at Trefelyn and whilst we were having tea there was a knock at the door. My aunt answered the knock, and it was the young lady I had spoken to earlier. My aunt asked her in and said "I suppose you have come to see the young soldier-boy as it's early for you to be bringing the milk". The young lady went red and was embarrassed!

I was at Garth House for 3 weeks, and then at Norton Fitzwarren. To get fully fit took 6 weeks and I was then posted to Newtown. In September 1945 following some home leave, I was posted to Gibraltar. I returned to the UK posted to Taunton Wrexham with the Somerset Light Infantry Band until I suffered a dislocated elbow.

Nursing staff at Garth House

I was sent to Chandlers Ford transit camp near Southampton next as a driver then back to Brecon once again. A few days later I was admitted to Chepstow Military Hospital, where they told me I had tuberculosis and was to be discharged from the Army. I had signed on for 7 years with colours and 5 years in the reserves and actually did 4 years and 109 days.

ALBERT THOMAS

ROYAL NAVY & CHESHIRE REGIMENT

Albert Thomas joined the Royal Navy as an Ordinary Seaman at the age of 18 years in March 1943. He trained at H.M.S. Raleigh in Torpoint, Plymouth and was then sent to Scapa Flow to join an auxiliary cruiser of around 10,000 tons, an ex-merchant ship called Dunluce Castle.

In peacetime the ship had sailed as a mail and passenger ship between Britain and South Africa. Within 3 months he passed his Able Seaman exams and after a gunnery course became an anti-aircraft gunner on board the ship which remained in Scapa Flow as a supply ship.

At the latter end of 1944 the war on U-boats was won and because there was a desperate shortage of infantry soldiers in Europe at that time Albert was transferred to the Army and retrained as an infantry soldier and joined the 1st Battalion Cheshire Regiment, which, together with the Hereford and Shropshire Regiments, formed the Infantry Brigade supporting the tanks of the 11th Armoured Division.

He drove an armoured car in C Company through Belgium, Holland and Germany meeting the advancing Russians at the River Elbe. The Cheshires continued through the Principality of Schleswig Holstein through Lubeck Kiel to the German-Danish border town of Flensburg. There they took the marine garrison where Admiral Dönitz and the remnants of the post-Hitler German government were located. He moved back to the Ruhr near Dortmund as Occupation troops.

Shortly after the 11th Armoured was broken up and the tanks, armoured cars and Bren gun carriers returned to Britain. Albert was transferred from C Company to HQ Company MT section and drove a Bedford QL 3-ton truck until he was de-mobbed in August 1947.

He lived in the *Railway Village* at the start of the war and remembers 39 men and one woman from those two rows of houses at Builth Road serving in the Forces during the conflict (from a total of 42 houses). One sailor, Doug Taylor, was killed in 1944 and Alf Evans died of illness whilst in the R.A.F.

EDDIE TURNER

LEADING AIRCRAFTSMAN (WIRELESS OPERATOR/MECHANIC) R.A.F.

In April 1939 conscription was introduced for single men aged 20 - 22 years. This was overtaken by the National Service Act when war broke out, covering men aged 18 - 41 years. By 1942 this was increased to 18 - 51 years for men and 18 - 30 years for women.

The calling up of older men meant there was delay for some of the younger men. While waiting we all did something: Home Guard, Air Raid Wardens, Observer Corp, Air Raid Precautions, Fire Service, Special Constables, W.V.S., etc. I was already a member of St. John's Ambulance, so automatically went into the A.R.P. - later changed to Civil Defence.

We had our headquarters in Broad Street, Builth between the Lamb Hotel and Queen's Vaults - now Mandy's Hairdresser. Two people were on duty all night. We were supposed to get the rest of the squad out of bed if the air raid siren went, but we never did, arguing that they would hear the raid anyway. The other terribly arduous duty was 'No cinema performance could take place without the presence of two Ambulance men'. No difficulty about volunteers for this job! We also had air raid drills - all dressed up in gas capes, respirators, tin hats, etc. Patients were labelled with their injuries. We occasionally bandaged the wrong limbs, etc., but again argued that if it were for real we would get it right.

Every week there was a full page notice in all daily newspapers giving instructions to those waiting to be called up. When your birth date was between certain dates and your surname started with certain letters you were ordered to register at your local labour exchange. In Builth this was in the Market Hall Buildings (now Wyeside). The exchange was between Mr Harry Davies' barber's shop and Mr Howard Lewis' (later Mrs Morson's) stationery and newspaper shop. The labour exchange was presided over by Mr Reg Walters. I duly attended, giving my full name, age and that I had not previously served in any of the Forces. There were a few other questions - education, etc.

Eventually I received a letter instructing me to attend for my medical examination. I was ordered to go to Pontypridd - most people went to much nearer centres. However, no arguing was allowed. I caught a train from Builth about 9.00am, changed at Three Cocks, Talybont and Dowlais Top, and arrived in Pontypridd in the middle of the afternoon, six hours later. A full medical and an interview followed. The elderly gentleman taking the interview asked a few questions, such as "Which service do you want to join?" I don't think your answer mattered - he had his instructions. Most of the people that day were miners with primary school education only; so Army. No choice there! Those of us who were more fortunate with secondary education did have some choice. I was, after a few questions, put down for training as a wireless operator in the R.A.F. Next day I had to go to Tonypandy for eye tests and then back home.

A two day job for something you would now do in an afternoon. My main memory of this trip was how many young men from the mining community were rejected with bad chests.

After another wait, a letter instructing me to go to Penarth Induction Centre arrived – at leat I think it was 'induction', but my memory is not clear on this. This time it was for three days, with further medicals, various forms, lectures and a maths test. I did not understand why I needed maths to learn Morse code, but apparently I did. We marched (very badly) from hall to hall. A few nights earlier there had been an air raid. A line of craters stretched across the cricket ground, and over the road a few houses had been demolished. The only remark made as we passed was "Good job they missed the square". At the end of this I was told I was now in the R.A.F. with the rank of Airman 2nd Class Wireless Operator Under Training (Wop/ut), with a number which, of course, like all servicemen, I still remember. Then back home for another wait.

Anson Mark II taxiing

October 1941, and a nice letter from His Majesty suggesting I report to R.A.F. Padgate. Being an obedient subject, I did so. I joined a number of others at the railway station and eventually we set off for the camp. On arrival large metal gates opened and let us in. They clanged shut behind us and we were truly in the service. Our journey to reception passed the station parade ground where we were greeted by the sight of two airmen jogging up and down, in full marching order, packs on back, etc. A warning!

After going through a few formalities we were shown to a billet. Next day we were taken to the stores and kitted out. This was quite a performance. We lined up and went to a long counter, and we then had a kit bag thrown at us, followed by all sorts of items. The following is a list (not complete – I've certainly forgotten something): 2 pairs of boots, 2 pairs of socks, a pair of gum boots, a pair of gym shoes, 2 pairs of pants and singlets, 2 shirts and 4 collars, a tie and a field service cap. In addition there was all the webbing (the various straps, etc. to attach the haversacks, etc.) with a belt, 2 haversacks, 2 ammunition pouches, a water bottle, a billycan, a knife, a fork, a spoon, a clasp knife, gas mask and gas cape, a ground sheet, a tin hat, a 'housewife' with scissors, cotton, wool and a needle. You stuffed all this into the kit bag or round your neck. Then you lined up and a corporal walked along and gave you a number, which you then gave to the W.A.A.F. behind the counter and she literally threw a jacket at you.

The same procedure was followed for 2 pairs of trousers and a greatcoat. I received my second jacket about 6 months later. You now had to get this lot back to your billet. Quite a performance! The corporal in charge of us then became very helpful, and those of us who listened to him did very well. A few rebels, of course, had a difficult time. We now had to mark every item we could with our name and number. We bought Indian ink and a pen from the NAAFI and spent most of the day doing this. Afterwards there were the usual lectures (the R.A.F. were good at lectures; I must have attended hundreds). We were taught how to salute and when. The saying "If it moves salute it, if it doesn't whitewash it" is not without foundation. Large pieces of brown paper, string and a label appeared. Into this we packed our civilian clothes which the R.A.F. then sent home for us. The big surprise for me was that my uniform actually fitted. The following day we were ordered to pack our kit and were marched to the railway station about a mile and a half away. Again, those of us who had listened to the corporal did all right; but there were a few who did not. One I remember, who spent the whole trip cursing the R.A.F. arrived at the station short of a few items. He would be in trouble later. Our destination was Blackpool. We arrived, and were now split into squads of 30 and remained in these until we left Blackpool. We were placed in civilian billets in the reception wing. The next week was lectures and drill. After this we were sent to billets we would remain in until we left Blackpool. I remember mine well – Mr and Mrs Miller. They did everything they could to look after us. Many of the boys were not so fortunate.

I had now been in the R.A.F. proper for a fortnight and it was pay day. We lined up in the usual fashion and a sergeant called out "Turner". I shouted back "Sir, 986", the last 3 digits of my service number, marched up to a desk and saluted. You then received your pay of 15/- per week (75p nowadays).

The next 3 months were spent: morning – Morse code; afternoon – drill or lectures. As it was December we had a lot of lectures and little drill. Blackpool front was not inviting in winter. As a bachelor I could do quite well on my 15/-. I went to a show most nights. Seats for servicemen were 1/-. What hardships we went through! The married men, however, did not do so well. They sent as much money as they could home.

After about 3 months we passed a Morse test. I cannot quite remember the speed, but it would have been about 14 words a minute. We went on our first leave, and then to Compton Basset in Wiltshire. Another 3 months Morse, drill and lectures. We now had to learn the R.A.F. procedure for wireless communication. Quite complicated. After 3 months of this we passed out as qualified wireless operators and were instructed to put the wireless operator badges on our sleeves. Some of us were then selected to be trained as 'Direction Finding' operators. This was the system used by the R.A.F. to help aircraft navigate before radar. It was surprisingly good and had been used by all air forces since 1917/18. When this course was completed we were sent on leave and then 'posted'.

R.A.F. airmen in India

I was posted to Carew Cheriton, between Tenby and Pembroke Dock. When I first arrived this was a Coastal Command Station, but in the process of changing to Training Command. So there was little to do. They had about three times the operators they needed. I got myself a job in the signals office - much better than potato-picking, which was the main occupation for unemployed airmen at the time. One morning the senior sergeant showed me an item in daily orders asking for volunteers to go for training as wireless mechanics. I remember his "This would suit you", and, of course, he was right. So, breaking the normal rules of not volunteering for anything, I applied. A week later I ended up at Cranwell in Lincolnshire - the Sandhurst of the R.A.F..

I was at Cranwell for the 6 month course, and, I must say I worked harder during that time than at any other time in my life. We were packing a 3 year course into the 6 months. However, it finished and I passed out AC1, which was very satisfactory. During the first months in Cranwell there was quite a lot of talk about a plane without a propeller which had flown there some months before. In about March, one weekend, there was great activity on the airfield and normal flying stopped. We then heard an unusual sound and saw a twin-engined aircraft without propellers taking off. I think this must have been the Meteor's maiden flight. I was quite pleased later when I realised I had been present at the first move by the R.A.F. from internal combustion engines to jets.

Again it was posting and when mine was announced it was to Carew Cheriton. This was something unheard of - returning to a station you had previously served on. I arrived at Carew knowing most of the people there. I was now on the staff of the radio school. This was quite different work, for apart from repairing equipment we equipped class-rooms, etc. I also spent quite some time at the transmitting station, and this served me well later.

British airmen in India 1944

"I still think Sergeant Edwards' early stuff is his best."

Eventually, of course, the posting came. A number of the school's mechanics were ordered to Chigwell in Essex. Since we were a group, we guessed we were heading for Europe. This was confirmed when we arrived. The next few weeks were spent in learning a number of new skills. I learned to cook on a field kitchen run by old used engine oil. This was in very cold weather and we enjoyed the results of our efforts. I also learned a lot about explosives and booby traps, particularly the kind the Germans used. However, no Europe. At one morning parade the corporal split the squad in two, according to the alphabet – 'A' to about the middle of the alphabet in one group, and the remainder of the alphabet in the other. Being 'Turner' I was in the second group. We were sent on embarkation leave. The other group, I understand, were eventually split and posted. One of them I kept in touch with, and he ended up in Norway. On our return from leave we were posted to Morecambe and our kit changed quite a bit. We handed in greatcoat, jackets and trousers and were issued with blue battledress and quite a lot of khaki. After all the time we had spent polishing buttons this did not go down too well. We exchanged one pair of boots and gum boots for mosquito boots. We also received a pith helmet (known to us as a 'Bombay bowler'). For the first time we were issued with firearms and ammunition. I had a Sten gun and 4 magazines containing about 100 rounds in all.

When all the preparations were complete we went up to Greenock and the Clyde, then on to a lighter and were taken out to the troopship "Orontes". When boarding, you received a card which gave your deck, etc. I was on H deck – pretty low down. A hammock was issued. One kit bag disappeared down a hold and you stored the rest as best you could. Hammocks were slung some 18 inches apart and staggered so your head was level with the middle of those on either side. It was quite comfortable, if rather crowded. Some did not like this and slept on the mess tables or on the floor. In a day or two the ship was full. One morning we went on deck to find we were at sea and apparently heading down the Irish Sea. During the next few hours we saw we had been joined by several other ships, including an aircraft carrier. I discovered many years later that one of the ships, a "Castle" boat, contained Mr David Jones, later National Provincial Bank manager at Builth. By the time we reached the open Atlantic the weather was bad. Sea-sickness took over. I did not feel too well, but did not suffer very much. Some people really were green. Looking at the other ships showed how bad it was. I was sorry for the Royal Navy men in the escorting frigates. Most of the time you could only see their masts out of the spray. The only duty I had was a 24-hour guard on the gun on the stern – 2 hours on and 4 off. At night you could not see anything, so what purpose it served I do not know.

We passed Gibraltar one afternoon. It looked quite impressive in the sunlight and the day after that we changed from blue uniform to khaki. We went through the Suez Canal and on to Bombay. We disembarked very early in the morning, and travelled through the city to our camp. Our first sight of India was of thousands of people sleeping on the pavements and traffic islands. Every space was occupied. After about a week at the transit camp we went on the train, travelling for a couple of days to a training camp in southern India. Here we went through the same programme as at Chigwell a month or so earlier.

"The cap, Sir? Well, you see, a helmet gives me a frightful headache!"

One afternoon a sergeant appeared looking for volunteers. Someone asked "What for?" and the sergeant replied "I don't know but I want 10 wireless mechanics". One of my mates said "Let's go, I'm fed up with this", so off we went again. When we got on the train we were told we were going to Karachi to service flying boats. We duly arrived, but the flying boats never did. So for a few months I serviced the wireless equipment on all sorts of aircraft, British and American. Then, the usual without warning – "Pack your kit and go to the transmitting station" – which was about 2 or 3 miles from the airfield. Here I joined a small team looking after the transmitters. This was the wireless station connecting London to India and Burma (South East Asia Command (SEAC)), so quite an important place. Wireless transmitters are quite straightforward compared with most receivers and already I had experience from Carew Cheriton. Everything was brought out to us and we did not move from there very often, and we were left alone as long as we did the job. They brought out our pay, but there was no point as there was not much in the desert to spend it on. We were so isolated we did not know the war was over until sometime the following day when the ration truck arrived. Eventually a message arrived that my demob number had come up. So, again, it was "Pack your kit".

The trip from Karachi to Bombay went via Delhi. We stopped so often and for so long that we were able to take a walk around a number of quite interesting places – quite a sightseeing trip really. There was a long wait doing nothing in the transit camp. Then we were on to the troopship "Alcantara" and home. We had another long train journey to the demob centre. Two days were spent handing in kit and, of course, another medical – this time to check you were fit to leave – what a change! We then collected a demob suit, pay and a railway warrant and off home. I now had 3 months leave due, so no hurry to go back to work. But after about 3 weeks I was fed up with messing about, so I returned to work.

I have still not made up my mind about this period of my life. I realise it took 5 years out of your life at quite a vital time, but I also know I quite enjoyed a lot of it. There was a lot of discomfort, bad food some of the time and a great deal of hard work, but it was always interesting. A number of friends were made and 'comradeship' is one of the things I will always remember about wartime service. During the first months at home I asked the question several times, "What's happened to so and so?", not always liking the answer. After my leave had expired I received a letter enquiring whether I would like to return to the service. I am still wondering if I should have. Bit late now!

Eddie Turner
Former holder of the exalted rank of Leading Aircraftsman (WOM – Wireless Operator/Mechanic) R.A.F.

TREVOR R. WILLIAMS 7927029

7TH QUEENS OWN HUSSARS

BY DAVID WILLIAMS & HELEN EVANS

My sister and I have put together some facts we know of our father's war service, he never spoke of what he had done for many years and then only bits and pieces or little anecdotes or having been somewhere or part of a campaign.

He was called up at the age of 33 which was quite old for front line service and before leaving he was offered a box of folded papers by a church minister and invited to select one. One paper seemed to stand out and it read *"The Lord will protect you";* this subsequently proved correct. After his basic training as a tank radio operator/gunner in which time they substituted Jeeps for the real thing as there weren't enough tanks for the front line let alone training. After basic training he was shipped to North Africa with the other recruits to join the armoured regiment who were preparing to stop the Italians who were driving all before them. Which is what they did until the arrival of Rommel and the Afrika Corps. The German Panzers and 88 mm artillery guns could hit our tanks at 1500 yards whilst our tanks' 2-pound guns had to be within 500 yards to reach them. During one battle in the desert he was ordered to change to a different tank, his original took a direct hit later in the battle. The army fought a withdrawal to El-Alamein from where the regiment were shipped to Singapore to face the Japanese who were pushing through Malaya.

Trevor Williams commanding a tank in the desert

Two days out from Singapore it was captured so they diverted to India to mount an attack through Burma from that direction. They were met with initial success but without proper supply lines they were forced to retreat, having to destroy most of their tanks, only keeping enough transport for the wounded and to pull some guns. They were faced with many hundreds of miles of jungle roads continually fighting off the Japanese, every man carrying what he could.

The Japanese were able to get ahead of the slow moving column and set up road blocks on several

occasions. They were able to use the guns to clear a way through. There were also Gurkhas with them who were brilliant at clearing the jungle. He had several lucky escapes, on one occasion in Burma he was relieved from his post by his replacement who arrived early. Minutes later the unfortunate soldier was shot dead.

Before leaving for war Trevor devised a secret code so his wife would know where he was; If he addressed the letter to Mrs I Williams this was India, Mrs E Williams was Egypt, Mrs J Williams - Jerusalem. In all they devised about 12 locations!

There is one story Dad told us when an officer was captured and tied to one of the road blocks. With no alternative the guns were ordered to fire and miraculously out of the smoke and flame came running the officer, blown free but otherwise unharmed. They finally reached British lines after many weeks of suffering terrible hardships. They were given R/R in the Murray hills but to get there the men were transported in cattle trucks, most being in such poor physical condition that half the men were in hospitals half across India with heat stroke, dysentery, etc.

During the retreat in Burma Trevor was missing for many months and strangely, one day whilst sitting in the kitchen of their home gazing out of the window, his wife saw a vision of many bedraggled soldiers, her husband amongst them, walking over mountains. From then on she knew he was alive.

By the end of the retreat and journey Dad was just over 6 stone. On recovering and the regiment ready for action they were shipped to the toe of Italy and fought their way up through the country by-passing Monte Cassino and arriving at the River Po and were preparing to attack across the river with high ground on the other side defended by heavy artillery which would have made for a very difficult and dangerous crossing when the army in Italy surrendered and the war was over for our Dad, Trevor Williams (Watts). Before returning home he and many other soldiers were granted an audience with the Pope. He asked Trevor where he was from and when told replied "Galles", the Italian for Wales.

Photo taken by Trevor Williams shows the British army in full retreat through Burma

David Willis

Sgt. 77/79 Batt, 6th Field Reg. R.A.

The Willis family lived in Builth Wells for several generations, once running several businesses in the town including the double-fronted grocery shop on Market Street, the White Hart Inn and a building, painting and decorating business.

David served in the Radnorshire Regiment (Territorial Army) and was called up for military service in 1939. David wrote the following letter on 7th May 1945 to his fiancée Eileen's parents who lived in Bebington on the Wirral.

Dear Mr and Mrs Sutcliffe,

We are all, like all the people in the British Empire, America, excitedly awaiting the official announcement by Mr Churchill that we can celebrate V.E. Day. For us at least the war is over in Europe, except for the final mopping up and occupation of Germany.

A few weeks ago, we hardly expected the end to come so suddenly, although the papers and, I hear, the people in Blighty expected victory any day. Some of the articles I read simply disgusted me. The advance from the Rhine and its crossing was simply a "walk over" by some of the papers. In my estimation the reporters who wrote such things didn't give very much credit to the men who took part in the action, or to those who fell. What I saw of it. The fighting was just as hard as any we've had over here, and I've been in every big campaign since D Day.

When the end came, it was as dramatic as anything written in a storybook. Never will I forget that day, on the advance from the Elbe. Everything seemed to happen in just a few hours. The Germans were on the run and as we passed through a village we met a couple of prisoners of war, who told us that Jerry had taken about a thousand British and American prisoners with them. In the next village those prisoners were waiting for us. They had disarmed their guards. What a marvellous welcome they gave us. An hour later our recce had met forward elements of the Russian army and then the Germans began to stream in, in thousands.

Whole divisions of them simply marching in and laying down their arms. Driving in, on any kind of transport, one lorry towing as many as three cars. Whole regiments of artillery, large and small, bringing their guns and hundreds of thousands of refugees running from the Russians. What a sight it was. A German officer, who spoke English perfectly, came up to me and said, "Will you please come with me, I wish to surrender my company". At first I was rather dubious about going with him, but decided to go with him. He took me behind a wood and there, paraded very smartly, were five hundred Jerries. The officer brought the parade up to attention and saluted, and I then told him what to do. I could hardly keep a straight face while all this was going on, because it all seemed so very unreal. Many other chaps had the same experience.

Since then I've been lucky enough to take a few snaps of the Russians, which I hope to have developed very soon. I hope they come out alright. It's hard to realize that there will be no more bombing of England. What a great relief the end of hostilities must be to the people of Southern England. The V bombing must have been a terrible ordeal.

All the chaps are wondering now when the demobbing will start, and for chaps like myself, who have served nearly six years, it can't come soon enough. All kinds of rumours are going around. One is, groups from one to twenty-four will be discharged by January next year. I hope it proves correct, because I happen to be in twenty-four group.

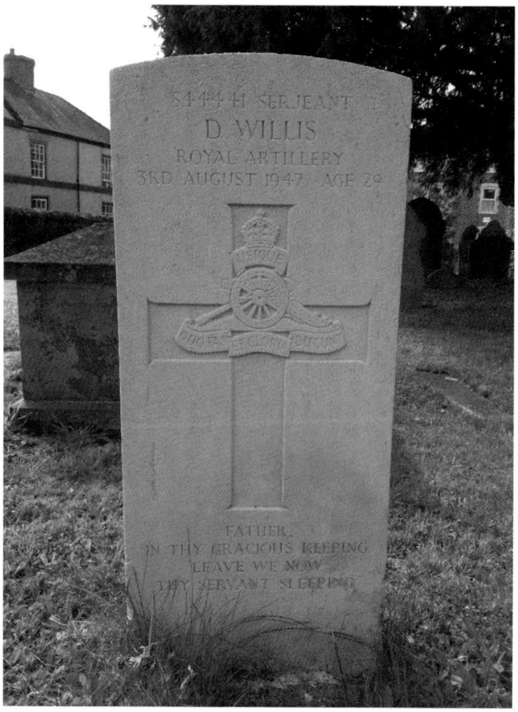

What the future has in store for us, I don't know, but I believe there will be plenty of work for us, in the building trade. Six years is rather a long time to be out of civilian life and I'll bet I will have a hard job settling down again. The army council have started correspondence courses in different trades and I think I'll single one out and try my hand at it. I haven't quite decided what to do yet, when I get back into civilian life but I don't think I'll go back to my old job with Reg. Perhaps I will have to in the end, but first I want to try my hand in another job, something much more interesting.

There are still the Japanese to think about and to be won, and by the news things are going very well out there. I suppose some of us will have to go out there, but I doubt very much if men in groups under thirty will have to go out. I've had enough of this army life myself.

What a change there is now the cease-fire has come. It's simply grand to go to bed at night with an untroubled mind, no more sleeping for months on end in trenches full of mud and filth. No more shelling to make a chap duck for cover and no more Jerry planes to worry us. It's great to be able to walk out in comparative freedom.

The news has just come through about V.E. Day being celebrated tomorrow. Well, I hope the people at home enjoy themselves but it will just be an ordinary day for us. We haven't a spot of beer or spirits to drink so it's going to be a dry day for us. I'll save my celebrating until I get home and then I intend to make "whoopee". My leave is due in June and, if everything goes well, I'll be home at the end of that month or the first week in July. Many things could happen by then though, the unit may even be back in England by then, but that's only a chance in a thousand.

Roll on June, and this time I'll book my passage to Liverpool and hope to have the pleasure of Mrs Sutcliffe spoiling me for the first few days of my leave. With your permission I will then take Eileen down to Builth for the remainder of my leave.

It's a year since I had the pleasure of seeing you and the last time it was under very different circumstances. D Day was very near and I knew it was the last time I would see you, for goodness knows how long. That short leave was very nice, but I could hardly enjoy it very much with so many things on my mind. The leave I had from over here in January was just the same and I felt it was my duty to spend the whole of it at home, although I would have loved a couple of days in Bebington. This time the circumstances will be different. It will be a peacetime leave again.

Please forgive me for not writing to you very often, because you'll understand how busy I have been and my spare time was spent writing letters to Eileen and home. My love to Brenda and Richard and I hope Brenda is doing well at school, also Richard at his job.

Hope you are all enjoying the best of health. When I have my leave Mrs Sutcliffe will have to come out riding with Eileen and I, on the bicycles!

The C.O. has just laid on a rum issue for the men in the morning, so we will have a V.E. Day drink after all. I'll be drinking your health tomorrow. Goodnight and God bless you all.

Yours very sincerely

David

We've "borrowed" a wireless set so I hope to listen to Mr Churchill's speech tomorrow.

David and Eileen were married in September 1946. At that time they were unaware that David, whilst serving in Europe, had contracted tuberculosis. In May 1947 he became seriously ill and was admitted to a sanatorium where tragically he passed away on August 3rd. He was laid to rest in St. Mary's churchyard, Builth. Following a request from his widow his name was added to the Builth Wells war memorial in 2012.

THE FALLEN

Many local men lost their lives during the conflict and are remembered on the various war memorials in the nearby towns and villages, the main memorial being the beautiful sandstone cross depicting a merchant seaman, Royal Naval seaman, soldier and airman situated in the town of Builth Wells. Other significant memorials are located in the Builth Cottage Hospital and in the many churches and surrounding villages.

In the following pages we remember many of the fallen that we have been able to identify who have connections to these parts.

Signalman **Ronald ASBERY**
2585088

Ronald Asbrey was a son of the family that once resided at Park Wells, once one of Builth's renowned spas. A member of the Territorial Army he was called to the Colours at the outbreak of war, and killed during the capture of Tobruk in present day Libya.

It is reported that a captured booby-trapped Italian field gun exploded. He is buried in Benghazi War Cemetery.

2nd Lt. **Lawrence Oliver MacKay BARSTOW**
124959 Royal Horse Artillery

Oliver Barstow of Chapel House, Builth Wells, was commissioned into "Mercers Troop", 5th RHA and served with the British Expeditionary Force in France in 1940, returning exhausted following the Dunkirk evacuation; after taking a bath he slept for a full 24 hours. Peter Fleming, (brother to James Bond author Ian) invited Oliver to join a sabotage mission behind enemy lines to blow up bridges, roads and railways to slow up the German advance. After many hilarious and sometimes ridiculous situations they arrived in Athens in time to evacuate the British Embassy. Surprisingly Oliver met his brother-in-law, the ambassador Sir Harold Caccia there. They received orders to leave for Crete immediately and that very night together with 80 embassy staff they left Athens under the noses of the Germans.

On the third day near the island of Polyagios they were attacked by a German Stuka and Oliver Barstow was killed manning a machine gun. The ship sank and his body was not recovered; he is remembered on the Athens Memorial. Oliver Barstow was a real hero and was mentioned in despatches during his Greek exploits.

Guardsman **Morley James DREW**
2737342 3rd Battalion, Welsh Guards

Died 26th July 1944. aged 30. Son of Owen and Gladys R. Drew, of Builth Wells, Radnorshire. Buried in Assisi War Cemetery, Italy. Plot VI, row D, grave 5.

Aircraftman 2nd Class **Alfred Edwards EVANS**
1279091 Royal Air Force Volunteer Reserve

Died 27th September 1943, aged 22. Son of Oscar Ralph and Maud Evans, of Builth Road. Buried northeast of the church in St. John Churchyard, Cwmbach LLechryd (or Builth Road), Radnorshire.

Master **Josiah Raymond EVANS**
Merchant Navy

Raymond Evans served in the Royal Navy throughout the Great War and he and his wife made their home in Querida, Garth Road, Builth Wells after the war. He became Master of a merchant ship "S.S. Coryton" where he spent 16 years. On 16th February 1941, following an Atlantic crossing in convoy, his ship struck a reef in fog sustaining severe damage and began sinking. The ship was beached near Holy Island, Northumbria, and all the crew were taken off by lifeboat, the Captain remaining overnight in worsening weather. Flashing lights were reported at 0630 on the 17th, apparently from the Captain's torch, but this was the last contact until his body was washed up on a beach. Captain Raymond Evans' body is buried in Builth Wells churchyard.

Pte **John Kenneth GLASSCODINE**
14989830 4th Bn. Welch Regiment

Son of the stationmaster at Builth Wells John Glasscodine was a member of the Air Training Corps before being called up for service in the R.A.F.; soon afterwards he was compulsorily transferred to the Welch Regiment.

On his 19th birthday in 1945 he was drafted to Europe and six weeks later whilst serving at Alpen, Germany on March 7th he died of wounds received whilst clearing the Reichswald Forest in some of the fiercest fighting .

He is buried in the Reichswald Forest War Cemetery.

Pilot Officer **Walter Samuel Palfrey GRIFFITHS**
61267 R.A.F.V.R. Bomber Command

Son of the Griffiths family who resided at Bryntirion, North Road, Builth Wells. Joined the R.A.F. in 1939 and became a pilot with Bomber Command.

He was shot down over St. Nazaire on 28th September 1941, aged 21. His body was washed ashore at Noir Moutier where he is buried at La Gueriniere Communal Cemetery.

Pte. **Edward HONEY**
14223132 1/5 Queens Royal Regiment

Born in Penrose, Raglan he moved to Builth Wells as a child and was educated at Builth County School. He worked as head draughtsman at Vickers Aircraft Manufacturing designing Wellington bombers and other aircraft.
Always eager to join the war he was several times rejected for military service due to the importance of his work.

Eventually his persistence paid off and he joined the QRR. Sadly he was killed (aged 29) by a sniper bullet in Duisburg, Germany on 5th April 1945, the day before VE day.

He is buried in Rheinberg War Cemetery.

Pilot Officer **David Vincent JAMES**
165383 R.A.F.V.R.

Only son of Mr & Mrs Charles James, (watchmaker), Builth Wells. Joined the R.A.F. and trained as a wireless operator in Canada, passed out head of section and was commissioned. On 25th November 1944 whilst on a training flight in the UK flying a "Mosquito" aircraft he was reported missing. His body was never recovered.

He is remembered on the Runnymede Memorial to those with no known grave.

Seaman **Llewelyn Albert JENKINS**
Merchant Navy

Son of Mr & Mrs J.A. Jenkins, Llewelyn served his apprentiship as a baker in Bristol House, Builth Wells, and later followed his trade on the S.S. Orama.

Following the outbreak of war his ship returned from Australia to Tilbury (via New York), and after a short leave his ship sailed to Narvik, Norway, to assist with the evacuation. Whilst returning to the UK the Orama was sunk by the German ships *Admiral Hipper* and *Han Lody.* Llewelyn Jenkins was reported missing, presumed drowned on 8th June 1940, aged 39.

He is remembered on the Tower Hill Memorial.

Pilot Officer **David Morgan Price JONES**
108245 R.A.F.V.R.

Born and educated in Builth County School where he was head boy and first editor of Wyeside Magazine, he went on to gain a degree at Aberystwyth.

He entered the R.A.F. in 1941 becoming a Pilot Officer Observer in 149 Sqdn. Following many successful raids on Germany he was reported missing during bombing operations over Belgium on 6th June 1942, aged 28.

Morgan is buried at Adegan Canadian War Cemetery in Belgium.

Flight Sergeant **Robert Henry McALPINE**
2221305 R.A.F.V.R. (Air Gunner)

Whilst dropping supplies to British troops crossing the Rhine on 29th March 1945, the aircraft radio malfunctioned and they returned to base for repairs. During a test flight over Peterborough following repairs a 'Spitfire' flew out of a cloud and collided with their plane.

Bob (aged 37) and all the crew died (including two young mechanics on their first flight).

Sergeant **John Leslie NEWELL**
2221305 R.A.F. (Fitter)

John Newell joined the R.A.F. in 1936 and served on H.M.S. Berwick during the Norwegian campaign. He was serving on H.M.S. Ark Royal when it was sunk off Gibraltar but was rescued and transferred to H.M.S. Audacity which unfortunately was also sunk in the Mediterranean on 22nd December 1941.

John Newell was 25 at the time of his death and is remembered on the Runnymede Memorial.

Signalman **Ivor Llewelyn William POWELL**
2335451 Royal Corps of Signals

Following a career with the Civil Service Ivor Powell joined the Royal Corps of Signals. He served in the Indian Signal Corps and spent time with the Chindits as a wireless operator behind Japanese lines in Burma.

He died aged 25 of typhus on 3rd September, 1944 and is buried in Imphal War Cemetery.

A.B. **James Bernard George PRICE**
Merchant Navy

Educated in Builth Council School, James went to sea at an early age and worked as a fireman and trimmer and was serving on S.S. Coryton under Captain Evans when it was sunk in 1941; he and two other Builth men (Trevor Lloyd and Geoffrey Owen) were rescued. James saw further service but was lost with all hands when the S.S. Baila was sunk on 14th February, 1942.

He is remembered on the Tower Hill Memorial.

Gunner **Jeffreys PRICE**
839426 6 H.A.A. Regiment, Royal Artillery

Born in Builth Wells he joined the Heavy Anti-Aircraft Battery, Royal Artillery in 1937 and was posted to Malaya in 1941.

He was captured by the Japanese at Singapore in 1942 he suffered great hardship, privation and malnutrition as a POW constructing the infamous Burma Railway.

He died in a prisoner of war camp.

Third Officer **William Thomas (Jackie) REA**
Merchant Navy

Serving on British armed merchant Fort Mumford, in the Indian Ocean, 500 miles NW of Ceylon on her maiden voyage.

The Japanese submarine I-27 torpedoed and sank them enroute from Colombo to Aden. The Mumford´s crew abandoned ship but Japanese Lt Cdr Fukumura complied with the Imperial "disposal" policy concerning POWs and ordered the slaughter of the Mumford crewmen by machine-gun fire.

The crew comprising 46 plus 4 gunners were lost apart from one survivor, a defensive gunnery rating, later rescued by an Arab dhow. Jackie Rea was 21 years old.

He is remembered on the Tower Hill Memorial.

Telegraphist **Douglas Percy TAYLOR**
D/JX 454425 H.M.L.C.T. (R) 457, Royal Navy.

Aged 19. Son of Percy Frederick and Dorothy May Taylor, of Builth Road, Radnorshire. His ship was mined off Ostend, Belgium on 5th November 1944. He has no known grave and is commemorated on Plymouth Naval Memorial, Devon, panel 88, column 3.

A.B. **Harold David TAYLOR**
Royal Navy Volunteer Reserve

Joined the R.N.V.R. and was called up at the outbreak of the war, serving on 'E' Class Destroyer H.M.S. Esk. The Esk had a very active war engaged in mine-laying and submarine detection and was awarded 3 Battle Honours between 1939 and 1941.

On August 31st 1940 aerial reconnaissance detected a German force and believing wrongly that the German ships were part of an invasion force, ships including the Esk were ordered to intercept. H.M.S. Express struck a mine and was badly damaged, H.M.S. Esk went to her assistance and hit a mine and sank immediately. Harold's body was washed ashore and buried on the German island of Pelwerm, and after the war interred in the Hamburg War Cemetery. He was 27.

Pilot Officer **Ronald Vincent TURNER**
65383 R.A.F.V.R.

Ronald Turner was the only son of Mr & Mrs George Turner of Oaklands, Builth. A talented musician (violin) and an active member of the local scout troop, he attained the 'King's Scout' award, he joined the R.A.F. in 1940 and trained as a pilot.

A skilled and experienced pilot he flew with 467 (R.A.A.F.) Sqdn, safely landing a blazing aircraft in 1942. He was killed during a bombing raid on September 3/4th 1943 and is buried in the Berlin 1939-1945 War Cemetery.

He left a wife, Elizabeth, and a daughter who he never knew.

Corporal **Alfred John VAUGHAN**
540407 Royal Air Force.

Died 28th October 1944, aged 25. He was the son of George Thomas Vaughan and Annie Jane Vaughan, of Builth Road, Radnorshire; husband of Lilian Vera Vaughan. He is buried in Alexandria (Chatby) Military and War Memorial Cemetery, Egypt, section O, grave 91.

4th Engineer **Robert James WALL**
Merchant Navy

Born in Cardiff, Robert came to Builth Wells to work at a local garage (Lewis Bros), and married a local girl.

In 1940 he joined the S.S. Bibury and sailed from Cardiff for South America. At 2204 hours on 30th August, on his first voyage, the German submarine U-46 attacked and sank S.S. Bibury and S.S. Thornlea west of Ireland.

Robert Wall's family received a letter informing them of his presumed death by drowning 2 months later.

Sergeant **Leslie Thorpe WATSON**
6340354 1st East Lancashire Regiment

Leslie Watson married Builth girl Mary Edwards and they lived in Market Street, Builth Wells. He was killed at Dunkirk on 1st June 1940 aged 31 and is buried at Pihen-les-Guines War Cemetery, Pays de Calais, France.